HIKING IN ANZA-BORREGO DESERT

Over 100 Half-Day Hikes

by Robin Halford

Illustrations by Paulette Ache
Maps by Jef Johnson

Published by
Anza-Borrego Desert Natural History Association
Borrego Springs, California

Library of Congress Cataloging-in-Publication Data

Halford, Robin
   Hiking in Anza-Borrego Desert : over 100 half-day hikes / by Robin Halford;
   illustrations by Paulette Ache; maps by Jef Johnson.
        p. cm.
   Includes index.
   ISBN 0-910805-13-X
   1. Hiking--California--Anza-Borrego Desert--Guidebooks. 2. Anza-Borrego
Desert (Calif.)--Guidebooks. I. Anza-Borrego Desert Natural History
Association. II. Title.
GV199.42.C22A5935 2005
796.51'09794'98--dc22

                                        2005048251

Editor: Betsy Knaak
Book Design: Scott Mayeda
Production Manager: Betsy Knaak
Printer: Thomson-Shore
Printed in the United States of America

The Anza-Borrego Desert Natural History Association is a 501c3 nonprofit
organization, established in 1971, dedicated to educational, scientific, historical and
interpretive endeavors that enhance the public understanding and appreciation of
the Anza-Borrego Desert region. ABDNHA's publications are an extension of its
educational endeavors. To find out more about ABDNHA's publications, programs,
special events, hikes and lectures, or for information about the Borrego Desert Nature
Center or membership in the Association, please contact the Anza-Borrego Desert
Natural History Association, P.O. Box 310, Borrego Springs, CA 92004-0310, (760)
767-3052, or visit our website at www.abdnha.org.

This book is dedicated by family and friends to the memory of David Cronshaw. Share in his love of this desert and its many hidden treasures.

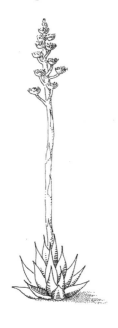

– The Anza-Borrego Desert Natural History Association acknowledges with gratitude the generosity of the family of David Cronshaw, without whose support this publication would not have been possible.

In honor of Art and Jean Morley, who lived and worked in the Anza-Borrego Desert for many years, and who have always been willing to share their extensive knowledge of the natural history of the area with those who joined them on walks, hikes, and field trips.

– Robin Halford, Author

CONTENTS

INTRODUCTION

Whether you are a first-time visitor or a desert devotee, this guidebook offers you access to the wonders of the Anza-Borrego Desert. Colorful peaks, scenic vistas and shady, narrow canyons await your discovery. Magnificent smoketrees and forests of cholla cactus and ocotillo inhabit Anza-Borrego's broad, sandy washes and sloping alluvial fans. By spending a few hours, half a day, or a lifetime, you can experience the great variety this desert offers.

Presented here are over one hundred short hikes within the boundaries of either the Anza-Borrego Desert State Park or the Agua Caliente County Park. Both parks are located in San Diego County in Southern California.

Anza-Borrego Desert State Park (ABDSP) is one of the largest state parks in the country, encompassing more than 600,000 acres (937 square miles). Anza-Borrego has both high and low desert areas that sustain a variety of plants and animals. The desert bighorn sheep, a favorite when spotted by desert hikers in the western canyons, is one of the animals protected within the state park. To see desert birds, look for places with a water seep or creek. To find the wildflowers for which this area is known, plan a visit during springtime, especially mid-February to early April. The spring wildflower bloom can be spectacular in years when the right weather conditions of rain and temperature occur. Cactus and desert perennial plants bloom dependably from winter into summer.

The state park has a visitor center in Borrego Springs and campgrounds throughout the park. The community of Borrego Springs sits within the north-central portion of the state park. Resorts, motels, RV parks, gas stations, grocery stores, and shops are available in the town. Near the center of town, the Anza-Borrego Desert Natural History Association, a desert educational organization and the publisher of this hiking guide, operates the Borrego Desert Nature Center, where visitors can obtain books, maps, and desert information.

Agua Caliente County Park comprises 910 acres. Located in the southern part of the Anza-Borrego Desert, Agua Caliente County Park is known for its natural hot springs, or *agua caliente*, Spanish for "hot water." During the desert season of fall through spring, the county park offers visitors naturally heated swimming pools and a campground. The park is closed during summer.

DESCRIPTIONS OF HIKES

For the purpose of making it easy to locate a hike within this large geographic region, maps and chapters herein organize the Anza-Borrego Desert into nineteen areas.

Within each area, each hike is described, including directions to the trailhead, distance, difficulty rating, terrain, and points of interest.

Distances are approximate to within a half mile.
1 mile = 1.6 kilometers, .6 mile = 1 kilometer.

Each hike description includes a paragraph with driving directions to the trailhead. Some trailheads are away from the paved road and may require driving on a dirt, or "jeep"road. For dirt roads, a vehicle with high clearance is always required and four-wheel drive is recommended. Access will depend on road conditions, vehicle type, driver experience, and vehicle load. Walking instead of driving may be required on these jeep roads. Check with park authorities for current road conditions.

A second paragraph within the hike description describes the hiking conditions. Some hikes follow jeep roads and can be shortened if a four-wheel-drive vehicle is driven part way. Features and conditions such as walking surfaces, topography, and dry waterfalls are included. Perennial plants such as cactus, trees, and shrubs are mentioned. Annual wildflowers are not seen reliably year to year, so not mentioned. The author has left many of the surprises for the hiker to discover and enjoy.

These descriptions are meant to help you decide which hike to take. Be aware that conditions vary from season to season and year to year. The effects of wind and rain constantly change the desert. An easy meander up a canyon becomes more difficult when a rockslide occurs; a walk up a wash can be on firm sand after a gentle rain or on soft sand after a hot, dry windstorm.

In the descriptions of hikes, the terms "wash" and "canyon" are sometimes used interchangeably. In general, a wash has walls that are lower than the wash is wide, and a canyon has walls that are higher than the canyon is wide. Both have been formed by water running downhill and forming a channel. Both washes and canyons are good places to avoid if there are storm clouds nearby, because flash floods do occasionally rush through without much warning.

JEEP ROADS

Most of the hikes begin from a parking area next to a paved road. Some of the trailheads are reached by driving on a jeep road. "Jeep road" is used here as a generic term for an unpaved road in the desert, which may be sand, dirt, rocks, or gravel.

Some of the hikes can be shortened by driving part of the way on a jeep road (or lengthened if you don't). When a jeep road is included in the driving instructions, then the road is usually passable by a two-wheel-drive vehicle with high clearance. However, a four-wheel-drive vehicle is always recommended. When jeep roads are included in the walking instructions, then four-wheel-drive vehicles are almost always required. Because the conditions of the jeep roads constantly change, it is always a good idea to check with the Anza-Borrego Desert State Park Visitor Center for current conditions. Four-wheel-drive vehicles may be required at any time of year.

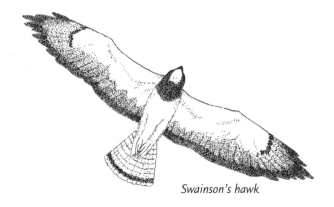

Swainson's hawk

MILEAGE & DISTANCE

DRIVING:

Many of the paved county roads have green mile-marker signs posted at regular, one-mile intervals. The signs can be posted on either side of the road. In this guide, mileage is given using the mile-markers whenever possible. Tenths of a mile are also included to give more accurate mileage. For example, Mile 4.3 will be found between mile-marker 4 and mile-marker 5. Using this mile-marker method is the most accurate way to find a parking area or turnoff.

Mileage is always given from one of four major intersections.
1. The Circle: the traffic circle in the middle of Borrego Springs, named "Christmas Circle," where Borrego Springs Road and S22 intersect
2. The intersection west of Ocotillo Wells: where Borrego Valley Road and Highway 78 intersect
3. The Tamarisk Grove intersection: where Yaqui Pass Road (S3) and Highway 78 intersect
4. Scissors Crossing: where S2 and Highway 78 intersect

This mileage is approximate, since odometer accuracy varies from one vehicle to the next.

WALKING:

Distances given for the walking sections are as accurate as possible and are given in tenths of a mile. However, conditions in the desert change constantly (i.e., a rockslide may require a detour or a flash flood may have changed the channel of a wash). Routes may have changed since this book was published. Also, one hiker may take a different route than another.

1 mile = 1.6 kilometers, .6 mile = 1 kilometer.

MAP LEGEND

▬▬▬	Paved road
～～	Unpaved road
••••••••	Hiking route along an unpaved road
···•••···••	Off-road hiking route
··•·····• P	Parking area
·····•··●	End of out-and-back hike
27 ∿	Mile marker
▲ 3052'	Peak with elevation (in feet)
🏠	Park building
	Area outside of park as shown on maps for hiking areas 1-19

OVERVIEW MAP OF HIKING AREAS

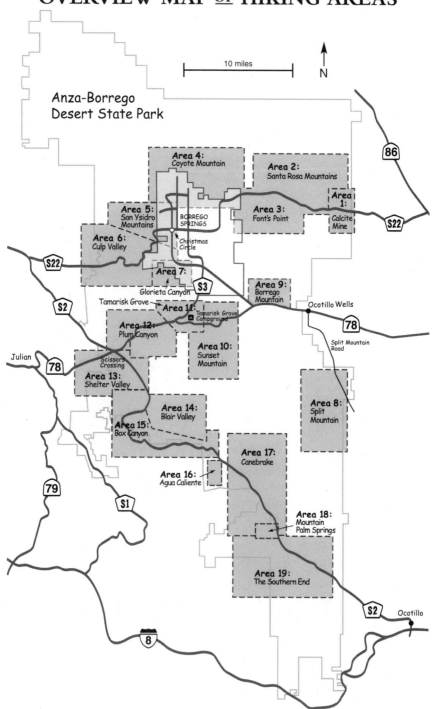

10 miles

N

Anza-Borrego
Desert State Park

86

Area 4:
Coyote Mountain

Area 2:
Santa Rosa Mountains

Area 1:

Area 5:
San Ysidro
Mountains

BORREGO
SPRINGS

Area 3:
Font's Point

Calcite
Mine

S22

Area 6:
Culp Valley

Christmas
Circle

S22

Area 7:

Glorieta Canyon

S3

Area 9:
Borrego
Mountain

Ocotillo Wells

S2

Tamarisk Grove

Area 11:

Tamarisk Grove
Campground

78

Area 12:
Plum Canyon

Area 10:
Sunset
Mountain

Split Mountain
Road

Julian

78

Scissors
Crossing

Area 13:
Shelter Valley

Area 8:
Split
Mountain

Area 14:
Blair Valley

Area 15:
Box Canyon

79

Area 16:
Agua Caliente

Area 17:
Canebrake

S1

Area 18:
Mountain
Palm Springs

Area 19:
The Southern End

S2

Ocotillo

8

LIST OF HIKING AREAS

LIST <u>OF</u> HIKES <u>BY</u> DIFFICULTY

Many factors can make a hike difficult: distance, elevation gain, type of walking surface, weather, and personal fitness. All hikes included here are rated according to the following scale to help you choose a hike that will be enjoyable.

FAIRLY EASY: Minimal incline/decline; possibly some soft sand and/or a few boulders to scramble over.

MODERATE: Noticeable incline/decline; some boulder hopping, uneven ground, and/or soft sand.

FAIRLY STRENUOUS: Definitely some elevation change with an uneven walking surface and some boulder hopping.

STRENUOUS: These hikes have very steep sections, usually with boulders or dry waterfalls that need to be negotiated, and the walking surface will be rocky in parts.

A note about distance: Many of the hikes are out-and-back hikes, where the hiker follows a route and then returns along the same route. Some of the hikes are listed as loop hikes. The Distance is the total mileage to be hiked, beginning at the parking area and ending at the parking area.

Distance: 1 mile = 1.6 kilometer; .6 mile = 1 kilometer

On the four Lists of Hikes by Difficulty that follow, the hikes are organized directionally, either from east to west, or from north to south.

FAIRLY EASY HIKES

| | Distances (total) | | | Description |
	Miles	Km	Area#	on Page No.
Badlands Overlook	1.6	2.6	1	15
Truckhaven Wash	3.6	5.8	2	22
West Truckhaven	2.2	3.5	2	22
Lute Fault Scarp	2.6	4.2	2	29
Vista Del Malpais	8.6	13.8	3	31
Corral Canyon	1.6	2.6	5	41
Flat Cat Loop	3.3	5.3	5	42
Hellhole Canyon Overlook	2.0	3.2	6	50
The Slab	4.6	7.4	6	52
Glorieta Wash	1.6	2.6	7	56
Elephant Tree Trail	1.0	1.6	8	59
Mud Hills Wash	5.2	8.3	8	60
Lycium Wash	6.4	10.2	8	63
Narrows Earth Trail	0.3	0.5	10	71
Nolina Wash Jeep Road	4.0	6.4	10	71
Mine Wash	0.2	0.3	10	75
Yaqui Pass Wash	2.0	3.2	11	78
Yaqui Camp	0.2	0.3	11	80
Bitter Creek Spring	3.0	4.8	12	87
Sentenac Birding Loop	1.2	1.9	13	89
Box Canyon	1.6	2.6	15	99
Bisnaga Alta	2.8	4.5	15	102
Palm Spring Loop	3.1	4.9	17	109
View of the Badlands	5.2	8.3	17	110
Southwest Grove	1.4	2.2	18	113
Egg Mountain	0.6	1.0	19	117
Bow Willow Wash	5.6	9.0	19	117
Dolomite Mine	1.2	1.9	19	118

MODERATE HIKES

	Distances (total)			Description
	Miles	Km	Area#	on Page No.
South Palm Wash	3.0	4.8	1	17
Cannonball Run	4.0	6.4	1	18
Moly Mine	4.6	7.4	2	27
Palo Verde Canyon	8.4	13.4	2	28
Font's Point	0.2	0.3	3	32
Borrego Palm Canyon	2.6	4.2	5	39
Little Surprise Canyon	1.2	1.9	5	43
Big Spring	1.6	2.6	6	47
Culp Valley Spring	0.4	0.6	6	48
Culp Valley Vista	1.0	1.6	6	50
Glorieta Canyon	1.0	1.6	7	55
Hawk Canyon	1.4	2.2	9	65
Slot Canyon	2.0	3.2	9	67
Old Borrego Valley Road	3.4	5.4	10	70
Powder Dump Wash	0.8	1.3	10	71
Nolina Canyon	3.4	5.4	10	72
Bill Kenyon Overlook	1.0	1.6	11	78
Yaqui Well	1.6	2.6	11	79
Stag Cove	1.6	2.6	11	80
Pictographs	1.8	2.9	14	96
Smuggler Canyon Overlook	2.8	4.5	14	97
Eco Road	1.8	2.9	15	99
June Wash	1.2	1.9	17	109
Maryís Grove	1.4	2.2	18	114
Palm Bowl Grove	2.5	4.0	18	114
Canyon Sin Nombre	3.8	6.1	19	118
Volcanic Hills Loop	8.2	13.1	19	119

FAIRLY STRENUOUS HIKES

	Distances (total)			Description
	Miles	Km	Area#	on Page No.
Calcite Mine	3.6	5.8	1	16
Primrose Path	2.8	4.5	1	19
Truckhaven Rocks	1.4	2.2	2	21
Coachwhip Canyon - North	3.6	5.8	2	23
Coachwhip Canyon - East	5.0	8.0	2	24
Rattlesnake Canyon	8.0	12.8	2	29
The Bench	2.0	3.2	3	32
Coyote Mountain	3.4	5.4	4	35
Hellhole Canyon	5.6	9.0	5	43
Calif. Riding & Hiking Trail	6.2	9.9	6	51
Oyster Shell Wash	4.0	6.4	8	62
Hawk Canyon Overlook	1.2	1.9	9	65
West Butte	2.2	3.5	9	66
Nude Wash	3.3	5.3	10	69
Quartz Vein Wash	1.8	2.9	10	70
Harper Flat	7.8	12.5	10	72
Bighorn Canyon	8.4	13.4	10	73
West Bighorn	4.8	7.7	10	74
Lizard Canyon-East Fork	0.8	1.3	12	83
Lizard Canyon-West Fork	4.8	7.7	12	84
Rocky Lizard	1.4	2.2	12	84
Plum Canyon	3.5	5.6	12	86
Pacific Crest Trail	9.8	15.7	13	90
Hornblend Canyon	3.6	5.8	15	100
Bisnaga Overlook	1.2	1.9	15	101
Moonlight Canyon	1.8	2.9	16	105
Inner Pasture	4.4	7.0	16	106
Squaw Pond	1.2	1.9	16	107
Torote Canyon	4.0	6.4	17	110

STRENUOUS HIKES

	Distances (total)			Description
	Miles	Km	Area#	on Page No.
Palm Wash Loop	3.2	5.1	1	16
Smoketree Tinajas	6.2	9.9	2	25
The Traverse	6.0	9.6	2	26
Alcoholic Pass	2.0	3.2	4	36
Third Grove	6.2	9.9	5	40
Panoramic Overlook	1.0	1.6	5	41
Borrego Spur	3.4	5.4	5	44
Pena Spring/Culp Valley Loop	8.8	14.1	6	49
Glorieta-Juanito Loop	3.5	5.6	7	55
Elephant Knees	3.6	5.8	8	60
Wind Caves	1.0	1.6	8	61
Ship Rock	0.7	1.1	11	77
Cactus Loop	1.1	1.8	11	79
North Pinyon Loop	4.2	6.7	12	85
Cool Canyon	5.0	8.0	13	90
Foot & Walker Pass	0.7	1.1	14	93
Ghost Mountain	1.6	2.6	14	94
Morteros Canyon	2.8	4.5	14	95
Rainbow Canyon	4.8	7.7	15	101
Desert Overlook	0.8	1.4	16	107
Torote Bowl	2.6	4.2	18	113
Mine Peak	2.0	3.2	19	119

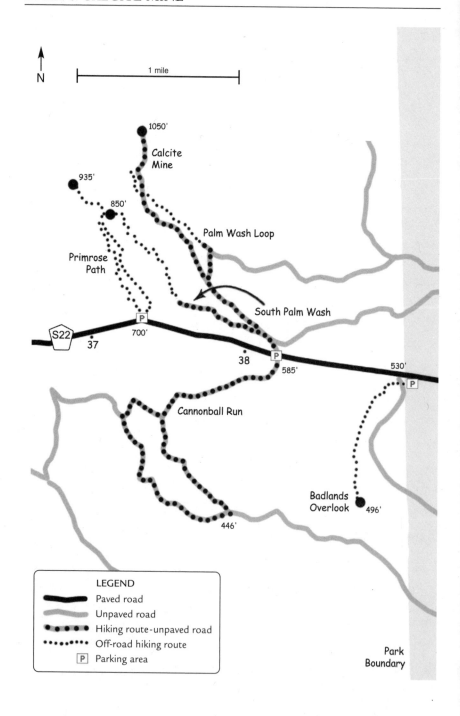

N

1 mile

1050'

Calcite
Mine

935'

850'

Palm Wash Loop

Primrose
Path

P

S22   700'

37

South Palm Wash

38

585'

530'

P

Cannonball Run

Badlands
Overlook   496'

446'

LEGEND
Paved road
Unpaved road
Hiking route-unpaved road
Off-road hiking route
P Parking area

Park
Boundary

AREA 1
CALCITE MINE

This area takes its name from the mineral calcite that was mined here during World War II and used to make precision sightings for guns and other weapons. The Santa Rosa Mountains to the north create a rainshadow effect, trapping winter storms on the mountains and dropping moisture in the canyons, leaving the desert floor dry. As a result, the canyons and washes in this area are a good place to look for spring wildflowers.

BADLANDS OVERLOOK
(1.6 miles total; Fairly Easy)

The parking area is at Mile 38.8 on S22 (approximately 19.1 miles east of The Circle), just east of the state park boundary sign. Park on the south (right) side of S22, directly across from the microwave station.

Walk past the "Closed Area" sign and along the abandoned jeep road that goes to the southwest for 0.5 mile. Look for ocotillo, creosote, saltbush, and silver cholla. The jeep trail gets very faint as it heads south for 0.3 mile to the edge of the ridge and a view of the badlands. Explore the area and then return the way you came.

Queen butterfly

CALCITE MINE
(3.6 miles total; Fairly Strenuous)

The parking area is at Mile 38.2 on S22 (approximately 18.5 miles east of The Circle). Parking is on either side of the road: look for the roadside phone on the south side of the road and the interpretative sign on the north side.

The trailhead is on the north side of S22 where the jeep road to the Calcite Mine begins. Walk down the eroded jeep road for 0.1 mile. Walk across South Palm Wash and continue up the jeep road another 0.1 mile to the top of the mesa. Follow the jeep road for another 1.6 miles to the mine area. Stop on the way to look at the encompassing view of Salton Sea to the east, Borrego Badlands to the south, Truckhaven Rocks and San Ysidro Mountains to the west, Santa Rosa Mountains to the north. The road is extremely eroded, and very few 4WD vehicles make the drive to the mine. Optical grade calcite was mined here during WWII for use in gunsights. Many cuts in the sandstone hillsides are still visible where pockets of calcite were removed. Return the way you came.

PALM WASH LOOP

PALM WASH LOOP (page 16)
(3.2 miles total; strenuous)
Follow the driving instructions for Calcite Mine.

The trailhead is on the north side of S22. The first part of the hike follows the Calcite Mine jeep road, which begins on the north side of S22. Walk 0.1 mile down the hill, cross South Palm Wash, and then continue up the jeep road for 0.1 mile to the top of the mesa. Look for cheesebush, saltbush, creosote, smoketree, desert mistletoe, and catclaw. Continue on the jeep road for 1.2 miles to where it crosses Palm Wash. Look for desert holly, indigo, brittlebush, and ocotillo. For a short side trip, go left (west) up the wash through a wonderful slot canyon. After 0.3 mile, the wash is blocked by large boulders, which are plugging the top of a dry waterfall. Walk back down the wash for 0.3 mile to return to the Calcite Mine jeep road. Cross the jeep road and continue walking down the wash in an easterly direction for 50 feet to a 4-foot-high dry sandstone waterfall, which is easy to slide down. The next 0.2 mile goes through a slot canyon with sandstone walls. Look for desert lavender, sandpaper plant, and desert fir. There is a narrow squeeze in the middle of this slot canyon. The canyon opens into a wide sandy wash. After 0.3 mile, look for the eroded jeep road that climbs out of the wash on the right (south) side. Walk up this road for 0.2 mile, and when it joins the Calcite Mine jeep road, turn left (east). A 0.5-mile walk will bring you to the parking area.

SOUTH PALM WASH
(3.0 miles total; Moderate)
Follow the driving instructions for Calcite Mine (previous page).

The trailhead is on the north side of S22. Walk down the hill on the eroded jeep road for 0.1 mile. At the bottom, turn left (west), and walk up the sandy wash for 0.6 mile to where the wash narrows. Look for desert mistletoe, cheesebush, saltbush, smoketree, creosote, ocotillo, desert holly, mesquite, and catclaw growing in the wash. Walk another 100 feet to a natural bridge over the wash. Walk under the bridge and continue up the wash for 0.3 mile to a narrow slot canyon that winds through 60-to-80-foot-high sandstone walls for 0.1 mile. There are a few low boulders to negotiate in the canyon. After exiting the canyon, look for coachwhip, sandpaper plant, brittlebush, and desert fir. The wash continues for 0.2 mile to a "hole-in-the-wall" among the boulders. Walk through this window and up the wash for another 0.1 mile. Stay left at the fork and walk 0.1 mile to the bottom of a dry waterfall, too high and crumbly to attempt. (The top of this waterfall can be reached from the Primrose Path hike.) This is a good place to take a break. Return the way you came.

Catclaw

CANNONBALL RUN
(4.0 mile loop; Moderate)

The parking area is at Mile 38.2 on S22 (approximately 18.5 miles east of The Circle). Parking is on the south side of the road: look for the roadside phone and the sign for Truckhaven Trail.

Follow the Truckhaven jeep road in a southerly direction for 0.7 mile and continue straight at the fork rather than going left. Follow the road as it drops down into the wash for 0.3 mile. At the bottom where Truckhaven Trail goes to right, turn left and follow the jeep road. Look for the concretions in the sandstone and mud hills on the left side of the wash. Some look like cannonballs. Also look for cheesebush, desert holly, brittlebush, creosote, catclaw, indigo, and smoketree. After 1.0 mile, turn right at the intersection, onto the North Fork jeep road. The jeep road goes through a wash that is full of beautiful smoketrees. After 1.0 miles, turn right onto the Truckhaven Trail jeep road which goes up and over the hill (no signs). Walk 0.5 mile to the park road marker where the loop began. Turn left and walk up the hill, and continue on the jeep road to return to S22.

Smoketree

PRIMROSE PATH

(2.8 mile loop; Fairly Strenuous)

The parking area is at Mile 37.3 on S22 (approximately 17.7 miles east of The Circle). There are wide shoulders on either side of the road just before (west) the low stone wall of the bridge, where the road passes over a culvert.

Begin on the north side of S22 and walk east across the bridge. At the northeast corner of the bridge, follow the path that climbs to the top of the embankment. Continue walking toward the northeast for 0.1 mile across the rocky desert floor. Look for a faint jeep road (abandoned) heading north. Turn left and follow this road as much as possible as it parallels the unnamed wash on the left side. Look for creosote, ocotillo, and saltbush. After 0.7 mile, the saddle at the top of the wash is reached. The upper section of South Palm Wash is visible to the north. Walk down the hill 0.1 mile to the west and then to the northeast to reach South Palm Wash. A short distance to the right is the top of the dry waterfall at the end of the South Palm Wash hike (don't get too close to the edge). Turn left and walk up the canyon for 0.3 mile. The canyon floor is sandy with a few boulders. Look for brittlebush, coachwhip, desert fir, catclaw, indigo, desert lavender, and cheesebush. Also, look for heart-leafed primrose during winter and spring. Climb through the "window" in the rocks, and then scoot up the right side of the big boulder. After another 0.1 mile, the canyon is impassable. Backtrack 0.4 mile and look for the trail on the right that goes up the saddle. Walk 0.1 mile up to the top and then another 0.1 mile down the rocky ridge. Choose a route on the right (west) side to drop down into the unnamed wash, and follow the wash toward the south. The upper 0.3 mile has many boulders. Walk through a squeeze in the canyon walls and then continue down the wash for 0.5 mile. This section is sandy with fewer boulders. At the culvert that goes under the bridge on S22, turn left and climb 0.1 mile up to the paved road.

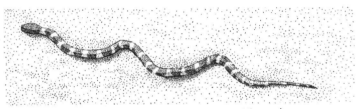

Kingsnake

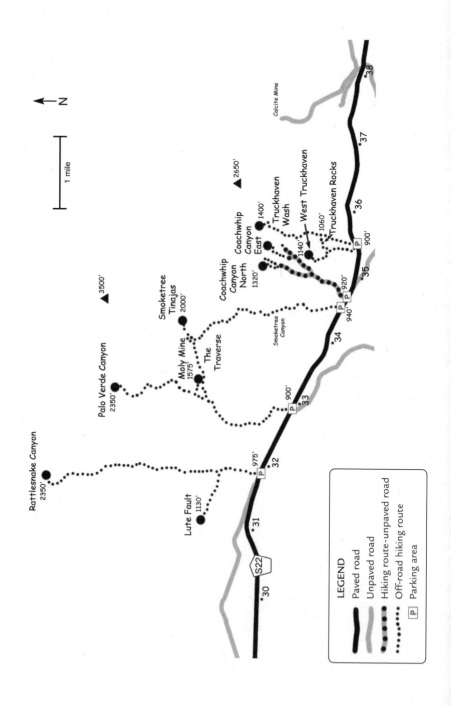

N

1 mile

Calcite Mine

•38

•37

2650'

Truckhaven Wash

West Truckhaven

1400'

Coachwhip Canyon East

1140'

1060'

Truckhaven Rocks

•36

Coachwhip Canyon North

1320'

900'

•35

920'

Smoketree Tinajas

2000'

3500'

Smoketree Canyon

940'

•34

Palo Verde Canyon

2350'

Moly Mine

1575'

The Traverse

900'

•33

Rattlesnake Canyon

2350'

975'

•32

Lute Fault

1130'

•31

S22

•30

LEGEND

Paved road

Unpaved road

Hiking route-unpaved road

Off-road hiking route

P Parking area

Area 2
Santa Rosa Mountains

The Santa Rosa Mountains are at the north end of the Borrego Valley. The canyons and washes on the south side of this range are dry and desolate, and the geology is different in each canyon. There isn't much vegetation, but smoketrees and palo verdes grow where there is underground water.

TRUCKHAVEN ROCKS
(1.4 mile loop; Fairly Strenuous)

The parking area is at Mile 35.5 on S22 (approximately 15.9 miles east of The Circle). There is a wide shoulder on the north side of the road where parking is available. (It is possible to safely turn around further on: Drive past the parking area 0.6 mile farther east on S22 and turn left, or north, toward the "point of interest" sign. Drive past the sign, turn right, or west, onto S22, and then drive 0.6 mile to the wide shoulder, which is now on the right side of the S22.) The parking area is in the wide mouth of a rocky wash.

Truckhaven Rocks rise above the desert floor directly to the north. Follow the wash for 0.5 mile as it goes toward the north, along the east side of Truckhaven Rocks (the Rocks). This wash is rocky in many areas so try to choose a sandy route where the walking is easier. Look for smoketree, desert lavender, indigo, cheesebush, creosote, ocotillo, and catclaw. After becoming parallel with the Rocks, climb out of the wash on the west (left) side. Skirt the south side of the Rocks and then walk to the edge of the next wash. It is 0.3 mile from the wash on the east side of the Rocks to the wash on the west side. Look for pencil cholla. Walk south along the edge of the wash for 0.1 mile until it is possible to climb down into the wash. Follow the wash, heading south, for 0.5 mile to return to S22. Look for brittlebush in the wash. The vehicle should be parked down the road to the east (left).

TRUCKHAVEN WASH
(3.6 miles total; Fairly Easy)

Follow the driving instructions for Truckhaven Rocks (previous page).

If you look directly north, you will see Truckhaven Rocks, which rise above the desert floor. Follow the wash that goes along the east side of the Rocks. This wash is rocky in many areas, so try to choose a sandy route where the walking is easier. Look for smoketree, desert lavender, indigo, cheesebush, creosote, ocotillo, catclaw, desert holly, and brittlebush. After 1.8 miles, the wash divides into several narrow and rocky canyons. This is a good place to turn around. Return the way you came.

WEST TRUCKHAVEN
(2.2 miles total; Fairly Easy)

Follow the driving instructions for Truckhaven Rocks (previous page).

Look toward the west to the low hill where the wash drains under the road on the north side of S22. Walk west to this drainage and then north up the sandy wash. Look for creosote, smoketree, cheesebush, ocotillo, desert lavender, krameria, indigo, and catclaw. After 0.5 mile, go left at the fork through a short narrow sandstone canyon. Look for desert holly, brittlebush, saltbush, and coachwhip. After 0.2 mile, walk another 0.1 mile through a slot canyon, and then turn right at the fork just after leaving the canyon. Walk another 0.1 mile and go right at the fork. Walk another 0.2 mile to a 5-foot-high dry waterfall and then to the end of the canyon. Return the way you came.

Roadrunner tracks

COACHWHIP CANYON - NORTH
(3.6 miles total; Fairly Strenuous)

The parking area is at Mile 34.8 on S22 (approximately 15.2 miles east of The Circle). Turn south onto the jeep road for Arroyo Salado. Park immediately. Walk west on S22 for 0.1 mile; cross to the north side of S22 and walk north along the jeep road for 0.7 mile. Look for smoketree, cheesebush, creosote, catclaw, saltbush, indigo, desert lavender, and brittlebush along the jeep road and coachwhip, desert holly, teddybear cholla and desert fir in the side canyons. Go left (north) at the fork and walk 0.5 mile to the next fork at the end of the jeep road. There are two ways to go here. Take the left fork and walk up a sandy and rocky wash with high sandstone walls for 0.5 mile until the canyon is filled with boulders. This is a good place to stop. Return the way you came.

Take the right fork and walk up the sandy wash for 0.2 mile to another fork. Go to the left and walk up a sandy and rocky wash for 0.3 mile until the canyon becomes filled with boulders. Or, go to the right and walk up a narrow, rocky sandstone canyon for 0.3 mile to an 8-foot-high dry waterfall. Return the way you came.

Coachwhip Canyon has many interesting features. The rock-filled canyons and eroded hillside formations are evidence of how much water can rush through this area during a storm. Most of the vegetation here occurs in the open areas of the washes. Not much can grow in the dry sandstone canyons.

Teddybear cholla

23

COACHWHIP CANYON - EAST
(5.0 miles total; Fairly Strenuous)

The parking area is at Mile 34.8 on S22 (approximately 15.2 miles east of The Circle). Turn south onto the jeep road for Arroyo Salado. Park immediately. Walk west on S22 for 0.1 mile; cross to the north side of S22 and walk north along the jeep road for 0.7 mile. Go right (east) at the fork and walk 0.4 mile. Look for smoketree, cheesebush, creosote, catclaw, saltbush, indigo, desert lavender, desert holly, desert mistletoe, ocotillo, and brittlebush along the jeep road. There are two ways to go at the next fork. Take the right fork and walk another 0.1 mile to the end of the jeep road. Walk up the narrow right canyon for 0.5 mile until the canyon becomes choked with rocks. This is a good place to stop. Return the way you came.

Take the left fork and walk another 0.2 mile to the end of the jeep road. Continue into the canyon for 0.7 mile until the canyon narrows and there are more rocks. This is a good place to stop. Return the way you came.

Coachwhip

SMOKETREE TINAJAS
(6.2 miles total; Strenuous)

The parking area is at Mile 34.5 on S22 (approximately 14.9 miles east of The Circle). There is a wide paved shoulder on the south (right) side of the road with room for several vehicles.

Cross S22 and walk north into Smoketree Canyon. The lower section of the canyon is wide with a sandy and rocky wash running through it. Choose the easiest route for the first 0.9 mile. Look for smoketree, desert lavender, cheesebush, creosote, catclaw, desert mistletoe, ocotillo, and indigo. Go left where two major washes combine. The canyon gets a bit narrower for the next 1.3 mile and there are more boulders to negotiate. Look for palo verde, desert fir, brittlebush, agave, teddybear cholla, barrel cactus, climbing milkweed, and ephedra, which early pioneers called Mormon tea. The canyon now gets very narrow with high rock walls and bigger boulders. Continue north for 0.7 mile to a 20-foot-high dry waterfall, which can be negotiated on the right (east) side. Continue up the boulder-strewn canyon for 0.2 mile. A narrow drainage comes down from the right (northeast). This is the beginning of a series of *tinajas*, or natural rock tanks, which are depressions in the rock caused by water rushing down the canyon and eroding the rock over time. Tinajas can be large enough to hold water year-round except during very dry years and are an important resource for bighorn sheep and other wildlife. Turn right and explore for 0.2 mile. Return the way you came.

Coyote

THE TRAVERSE

(6.0 miles one way; Strenuous)

The easiest way to do this hike is to arrange a car shuttle using two vehicles. Drive both vehicles to Mile 34.5 on S22 (approximately 14.9 miles east of The Circle). There is a wide paved shoulder on the south (right) side of the road, opposite Smoketree Wash. Park one vehicle here. Put all people and gear into the second vehicle and drive west on S22 to Mile 32.9. Park on the south (left) side of the road near the sign for Palo Verde Wash. Remember to take the keys for the first vehicle.

Look across the paved road (S22) to the northwest where several palo verde trees grow next to the road. Cross S22 and walk toward these trees, which are in Palo Verde Wash. This wash is well named, as there are many healthy green palo verde trees growing in the wash and canyon, but not beyond. Follow the trees in the sandy and rocky wash that goes in a north-by-northwest direction. After 0.3 mile, the wash cuts between two low mud hills. Now follow the wash as it turns toward the west and skirts the north side of one of the mud hills. After 0.3 mile, near the west end of the hill, the wash turns to the north. This section of the wash is very wide, so pick the best route available. Look for smoketree, creosote, indigo, pencil cholla, teddybear cholla, and barrel cactus. After 0.9 mile, the wash begins to narrow. Stay near the ridge on the right side of the wash. After another 0.3 mile, look for the palo verde tree on the right with several rock cairns next to it that mark the beginning of the traverse trail. Turn right and follow this faint, rocky trail as it climbs steeply up the south side of a drainage from the east. After 0.2 mile, Moly Mine will be visible on the north side of the drainage. Continue to follow the faint trail as it climbs another 0.5 mile to the saddle. Look for brittlebush and ocotillo. From the top, Lute Fault Scarp and the north end of the Borrego Valley are visible to the west and Smoketree Canyon is visible to the east. Follow the faint trail for another 0.5 mile as it descends into Smoketree Canyon. Turn right and follow the canyon for 0.3 mile to the top of a dry waterfall, which can be negotiated on the left (east) side. Continue down the narrow boulder-strewn canyon for 0.5 mile to where the canyon widens. The next 0.5 mile has fewer boulders and many desert lavenders. Then the canyon widens even more. The next 1.7 miles supports many smoketrees in the sandy, rocky wash. The first vehicle will be at the mouth of the wash, on the south side of S22. Drive west on S22 to pick up the second vehicle parked at Palo Verde Wash.

MOLY MINE
(4.6 miles total; Moderate)

The parking area is at Mile 32.9 on S22 (approximately 13.4 miles east of The Circle). On the south side of the road is a sign for Palo Verde Wash. Park near the sign and the huge palo verde tree near the road.

Look across the paved road (S22) to the northwest where several palo verde trees grow next to the road. Cross S22 and walk toward these trees located in Palo Verde Wash. This wash is well named, as there are many healthy green palo verde trees growing in the wash and canyon, but not beyond. Follow the trees in the sandy and rocky wash that goes in a north-by-northwest direction. After 0.3 mile, the wash cuts between two low mud hills. Now follow the wash as it turns toward the west and skirts the north side of one of the mud hills. After 0.3 mile, near the west end of the hill, the wash turns to the north. This section of the wash is very wide, so pick the best route available. Look for smoketree, creosote, indigo, pencil cholla, teddybear cholla, and barrel cactus. After 0.9 mile the wash begins to narrow. After another 0.5 mile, the wash narrows even more, and there is a large patch of exposed white rock on the left hillside. Walk around the rock outcrop on the right side and look for a faint trail that goes up the hillside on the right side of the wash. This 0.3-mile trail goes to the Moly Mine. [Warning: do not enter abandoned mine shafts.] The geology in this canyon is fascinating. Be sure to notice the varied colors and sedimentation in the hillsides. Return the way you came.

Barrel cactus

PALO VERDE CANYON
(8.4 miles total; Moderate)

Follow the driving instructions for Moly Mine (previous page).

Look across the paved road (S22) to the northwest where several palo verde trees grow next to the road. Cross S22 and walk toward these trees located in Palo Verde Wash. This wash is well named as there are many healthy green palo verde trees growing in the wash and canyon, but not beyond. Follow the trees in the sandy and rocky wash that goes in a north-by-northwest direction. After 0.3 mile, the wash cuts between two low mud hills. Now follow the wash as it turns toward the west and skirts the north side of one of the mud hills. After 0.3 mile, near the west end of the hill, the wash turns to the north. This section of the wash is very wide, so pick the best route available. Look for smoketree, creosote, indigo, pencil cholla, teddybear cholla, and barrel cactus. After 0.9 mile, the wash begins to narrow. After another 0.5 mile, the wash narrows even more, and there is a large patch of exposed white rock on the left hillside and a rock outcrop on the right side of the canyon. Continue walking up the canyon toward the east for 0.4 mile. The canyon then turns toward the north. Look for desert fir, catclaw, smoketree, agave, and desert lavender. Follow the canyon for another 1.8 miles to where the canyon ends in an amphitheater. Enjoy the narrow view of the San Ysidro Mountains to the west and then return the way you came.

Desert iguana

LUTE FAULT SCARP
(2.6 miles total; Fairly Easy)

The parking area is at Mile 31.9 on S22 (approximately 12.4 miles east of The Circle). The parking area is on the north side of S22 near a roadside phone. Look to the north and locate a low ridge one-half mile away, rising to the west. Walk 0.5 mile through a sandy area out to the toe of this ridge, and then walk 0.7 mile up the slope to the top. Look for ocotillo, creosote, cheesebush, agave, brittlebush, and teddybear cholla. Walk another 0.1 mile to reach two survey markers. Look for a can with a sign-in book next to one of the markers. The escarpment on the north side of Lute Ridge rises 100 feet above the desert floor and is part of the Clark Fault, which runs through Rockhouse Canyon to the northwest and Arroyo Salado to the southeast. Rattlesnake Canyon is directly to the north. Return the way you came.

RATTLESNAKE CANYON
(8.0 miles total; Fairly Strenuous)

Follow the driving instructions for Lute Fault Scarp.

Look to the north and locate a low ridge one-half mile away, rising to the west. Walk 0.5 mile through a sandy area out to the toe of this ridge. Keep the toe on your left and continue walking north another 0.5 mile over a rocky area to the mouth of Rattlesnake Canyon. Drop down into the wash and walk up the wash 0.5 mile to a 10-foot-high dry waterfall, which is easy to negotiate on the right side. Continue walking in a northerly direction up the rocky and sandy floor of the canyon. Look for ocotillo, cheesebush, agave, brittlebush, creosote, teddybear cholla, barrel cactus, and climbing milkweed. After 2.5 miles the canyon forks. Take the right fork, which quickly ends at a steep 20-foot-high dry waterfall. This is a good place to stop. Return the way you came.

29

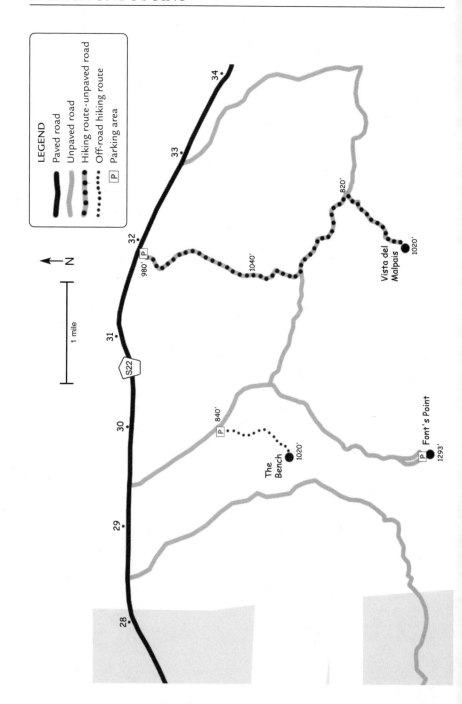

Area 3
Font's Point

Font's Point is one of the most recognized geographic features from Borrego Springs. It is also one of the most accessible vantage points for viewing the rugged Borrego Badlands. Other places in this section also offer good views of the badlands.

VISTA DEL MALPAIS
(8.6 miles total; Fairly Easy)

The parking area is at Mile 31.9 on S22 (approximately 12.4 miles east of The Circle). The parking area is on the south side of S22, across the road from a roadside phone.

Follow the jeep road south for 2.0 miles as it rolls over the dunes and hills above the Borrego Badlands. There are views of the badlands along this stretch. Look for ocotillo, creosote, saltbush, krameria, burrobush, and silver cholla. At the intersection with Short Wash jeep road, turn left (east) and walk for 0.1 mile, and then the road drops down into Short Wash. Continue east on the jeep road as it travels through the wash for 1.2 miles. Look for brittlebush, desert holly, and indigo. Turn right at the next intersection and walk 0.1 mile, and then stay south (left) and walk 1.0 mile to Vista del Malpais. The view of the badlands is spectacular, with Font's Point visible to the west. Return the way you came.

THE BENCH
(2.0 total; Fairly Strenuous)

From The Circle in Borrego Springs, drive east on S22 to Mile 29.4 (approximately 10.0 miles). Turn right (south) onto the jeep road for Font's Point. Drive up the wide, sandy wash and look for smoketree and desert willow, these trees are evidence of underground water in this area. After 1.1 miles, look for a wash on the right (west) side with a brown metal state park sign that says "CLOSED AREA, No Motor Vehicles." Park here on hard-packed sand.

Walk west past the metal sign and continue up this side wash. Look for alkali goldenbush, indigo, creosote, desert holly, saltbush, ocotillo, and burroweed. After 0.7 mile, the wash narrows slightly and then forks. The Bench is visible to the west on the top of a hill. Take the right fork and walk 0.2 mile toward this hill. Pick a route and walk 0.1 mile to the top of the hill and the manmade sandstone bench. Enjoy the view of the Santa Rosa Mountains and Clark Dry Lake to the north and the Borrego Badlands to the west, south, and east. The 1,600 acres surrounding The Bench were donated to Anza-Borrego Desert State Park in 1974. Return the way you came.

FONT'S POINT
(0.2 mile total; Moderate)

From The Circle in Borrego Springs, drive east on S22 to Mile 29.4 (approximately 10.0 miles). Turn right (south) onto the jeep road for Font's Point. Drive up the wide, sandy wash and look for smoketree and desert willow, trees that require underground water to survive in this area. Drive south for 3.8 miles and park at the end of the road, near the gray boulders.

Walk south up the well-worn path for 0.1 mile to near the edge of the cliff (don't get too close). This is one of the best views of the Borrego Badlands. At any time of day, the ruggedness of this topography is easily seen. The Salton Sea is visible to the east, the Santa Rosa Mountains to the north, and the Borrego Valley to the west. Return the way you came.

NOTES

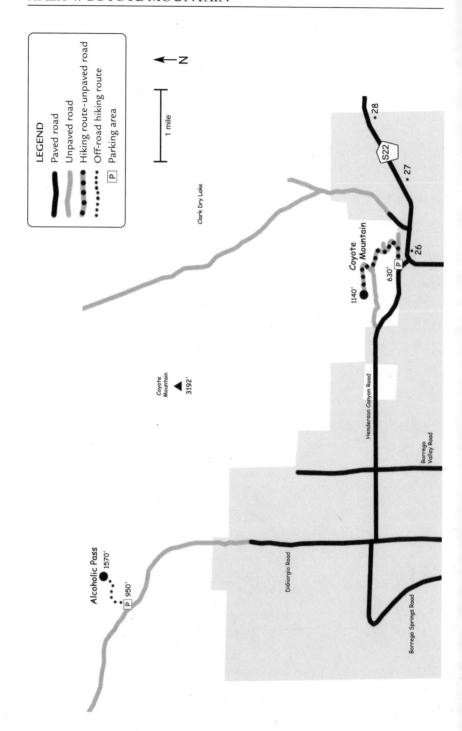

AREA 4
COYOTE MOUNTAIN

Coyote Mountain is part of the Santa Rosa Mountains and is one of the prominent landmarks visible from Borrego Springs. From a distance, the mountainside looks smooth. Up close, the terrain is steep and rocky with deep canyons cutting across the ridgeline.

COYOTE MOUNTAIN
(3.4 miles or more total; Fairly Strenuous)

From The Circle in Borrego Springs, drive east and then north on S22 (Palm Canyon Drive) for 5.0 miles. At Mile 25.8, turn left onto Henderson Canyon Road and drive 0.1 mile. Turn right into the Pegleg Monument dry camp. Drive to the north end and park next to the historical marker.

Follow the abandoned jeep road directly east for 0.2 mile and then go left at the fork. Continue to follow the jeep road as it climbs up the rocky toe of Coyote Mountain. Look for creosote, ocotillo, and teddybear cholla. After 0.9 mile, go right at the fork. Another 0.6 mile will bring you to a rock cairn. There are good views of the Borrego Valley from this point. This is a good place to stop. (It is possible to continue to follow the jeep road, which goes for miles further up the mountain.) Return the way you came.

Bobcat

ALCOHOLIC PASS
(2.0 miles total; Strenuous)

From The Circle in Borrego Springs, drive east on S22 (Palm Canyon Drive) for 0.5 mile. Turn left onto DiGiorgio Road and drive north for 4.7 miles. When the pavement ends, continue north and then northwest along the base of Coyote Mountain on the jeep road for 2.4 miles. Park by the marker for Alcoholic Pass on the right side of the road.

Walk north along the base of the hill for 0.2 mile. Look for ocotillo, saltbush, indigo, creosote, buckhorn cholla, teddybear cholla, brittlebush, barrel cactus, prickly pear, and krameria. Look for the trail marker and well-worn trail going up the hillside. Follow the steep, rocky trail for 0.5 mile. Then the trail levels off for the next 0.3 mile to the pass where there is a sign-in book. This is a good place to stop. This trail has great views of the mouth of Coyote Canyon and the north end of Borrego Springs. (It is possible to continue walking over the saddle and down the wash on the east side of the pass. This section is Moderate in difficulty, and will add 2.5 miles, one way, from the sign-in box to the jeep road in Clark Dry Lake. Look for desert lavender, catclaw, pencil cholla, and jojoba.) Return the way you came.

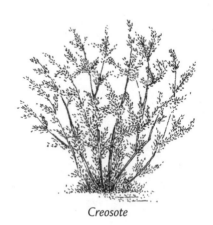

Creosote

NOTES

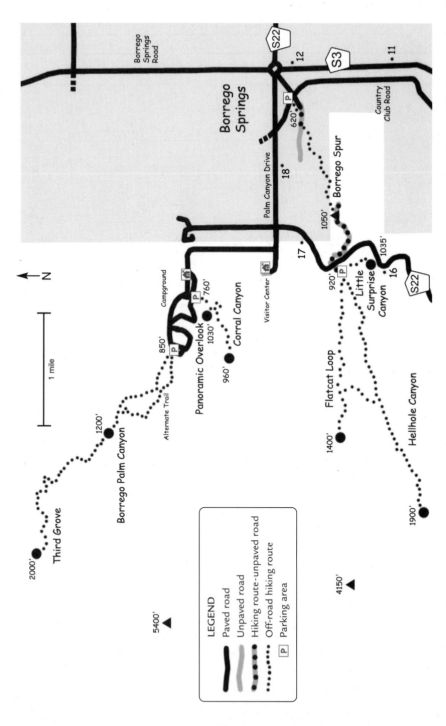

AREA 5
SAN YSIDRO MOUNTAINS

These mountains form the western boundary of the Borrego Valley and a weather transition zone. Most storms don't make it all the way over these mountains, creating a rainshadow effect. The moisture is dropped on the mountains, and the desert floor is usually left dry. The eastern edge of these mountains is striated with canyons and alluvial fans.

BORREGO PALM CANYON
(~~2.6~~ 3.0 mile loop; Moderate)

12-21-07
W/CHARLIE
3 HRS.

From The Circle in Borrego Springs, drive west on S22 (Palm Canyon Drive) for 1.5 miles. Turn right (north) and follow the signs for 0.9 mile to Borrego Palm Canyon Campground. The parking area is at the base of the mountain, 0.9 mile past the kiosk entrance to the campground. This is the most popular hike in the state park.

Borrego Palm Canyon has been affected in recent years by powerful flash floods from summer rains. This trail has been washed out in several places, but the objective is the same as in past years: to walk up the canyon to the native palm grove and then return.

The trail begins next to the information sign near the east side of the parking lot. Walk north along the existing trail of 0.1 mile. Drop down into the wash, and walk toward the northwest and across the wash for 0.2 mile. Walk up the canyon on the right (north) side of the drainage for 0.5 mile. Look for ironwood, ocotillo, creosote, desert lavender, desert mistletoe, cheesebush, and chuparosa. When the canyon turns toward the west (left), look for wooden marker #12 on the south side of the canyon. Cross over to this marker, turn right, and follow the trail toward the west. Look for mesquite, catclaw, and California fan palm. After 0.4 mile, there is a small palm grove next to a waterfall. Stop here to look for birds attracted to the permanent water in this area. Backtrack 0.4 mile to marker #12. Continue straight on the "alternate" trail, which has not been affected by the floods. Look for buckhorn cholla, krameria, brittlebush, ephedra (Mormon tea), and indigo. Stop occasionally to look at the view of Borrego Valley. Walk 1.0 mile to

THIRD GROVE

(6.2 miles total; Strenuous)

Follow the driving instructions for Borrego Palm Canyon (previous page).

The trail begins next to the information sign near the east end of the parking lot. Follow the walking instruction for Borrego Palm Canyon for 1.2 miles to the waterfall in the first grove of native palm trees. Walk back 100 feet to the trail on the east side of the huge boulder. Follow this trail up to the north and then toward the west for 0.2 mile to reach the end of the first grove. Continue walking up the canyon for 0.4 mile to reach the beginning of the second grove. Walk 1.0 mile to the end of the second grove. Walk 0.1 mile to the beginning of the third grove and then another 0.2 mile to reach the end. Return the way you came.

California fan palms

PANORAMIC OVERLOOK
(1.0 mile total; Strenuous)

From The Circle in Borrego Springs, drive west on S22 (Palm Canyon Drive) for 1.5 miles. Turn right (north) and follow the signs 0.9 mile to Borrego Palm Canyon Campground. Drive past the kiosk, take the first left and follow the signs for 0.2 mile to space #71 in the campground. Park in the area next to the three palm trees.

Walk southwest along the base of the hill for 0.2 mile. Look for indigo, creosote, krameria, ocotillo, brittlebush and buckhorn cholla. Watch for the sign to the overlook, where the trail begins to steeply switchback up the hill. Walk 0.3 mile to reach the top. There are excellent views of Borrego Palm Canyon Campground, the town of Borrego Springs, the surrounding valley, and Font's Point. The canyon on the south side is Corral Canyon. Return the way you came.

CORRAL CANYON
(1.6 mile total; Fairly Easy)

Follow the driving instructions for Panoramic Overlook.

Walk southwest along the base of the hill. Continue past the sign for the overlook and around the base of the hill. Walk up the sandy wash in a westerly direction. About 0.5 mile from the trailhead, the wash divides. Take the left branch, which is an easier walk. After 0.3 mile, the wash narrows and gets steeper with more boulders and fewer sandy patches. Look for brittlebush, indigo, ocotillo, creosote, chuparosa, desert lavender, and catclaw. (For a longer and more strenuous hike, and for good views of the Borrego Valley, continue up the canyon for another 0.5 mile to the top of the white outcrop.) Return the way you came. In the early 1970s, park rangers kept a horse in a corral here, which is how this canyon got its local name.

Snake tracks

FLAT CAT LOOP
(3.3 miles total; Fairly Easy)

From The Circle in Borrego Springs, drive west on S22 (Palm Canyon Drive) for 1.3 miles. Turn left onto S22 (Montezuma Valley Road) and drive south for 0.8 mile. Look for the information sign and turn right (west) into the Hellhole Canyon parking area. Park near the information sign.

Stand next to the vehicle and look to the west. There are several canyons coming down from the San Ysidro Mountains. The canyon that is furthest to the south (left) is Hellhole Canyon. The next canyon to the north (right) is Flat Cat Canyon. This canyon looks very steep and full of boulders, which it is. Near the top, the canyon turns to the right and around the back of a ridge. The tops of a few native fan palms are visible at this turn. A fairly easy hike is possible by just going to the mouth of the canyon.

To begin, walk across the desert toward the west for 1.2 miles, in the direction of Flat Cat Canyon. Look for indigo, cheesebush, creosote, ocotillo, buckhorn cholla, teddybear cholla, jojoba, desert lavender, hedgehog cactus, brittlebush, chuparosa, agave, and catclaw. Cross the dry wash that runs southwest to northeast along the base of the mountains. Continue west toward the canyon, following the drainage from the canyon. After 0.2 mile, the drainage becomes choked with boulders. This is a good place to stop and enjoy the view of the Borrego Valley to the east. Walk down the drainage, retracing your steps for 0.2 mile to the wash running along the base of the mountains. At the wash, turn right (southwest) and follow the wash for 0.4 mile toward the mouth of Hellhole Canyon. Look for desert willow in the wash, evidence of underground water. When the wash gets very close to the ridge to the south, turn left and climb out of the wash. Walk over the low berm toward the ridge to the south (approximately 25 yards) to the Hellhole Canyon trail. Turn left and walk down the trail, toward the east. The parking area will be reached after 1.3 miles.

HELLHOLE CANYON
(5.6 miles total; Fairly Strenuous)

Follow the driving instructions for Flat Cat Loop (previous page).

The trail begins near the information board. Walk west for 1.3 miles up a well-worn, sandy trail to the mouth of the canyon. Look for creosote, indigo, cheesebush, ocotillo, brittlebush, chuparosa, buckhorn cholla, agave, sage, jojoba, prickly pear, teddybear cholla, ephedra, barrel cactus, desert willow, desert apricot, hedgehog, and desert lavender. The vegetation in the canyon was burned by a fire in 2002, so pick the best route available through the new growth. Walk up the canyon for 0.8 mile to an oasis with palm trees and sycamores. Look for sugarbush. After another 0.7 mile of scrambling over boulders, look for the grotto. Water seeps and drips down the rock wall making it possible for mosses and maidenhair ferns to grow here year-round. At times, a waterfall flows down the rock wall. Return the way you came.

LITTLE SURPRISE CANYON
(1.2 miles total; Moderate)

Follow the driving instructions Flat Cat Loop (previous page).

Begin on the west side of the restrooms and walk south into the canyon that parallels Montezuma Valley Road. After 0.1 mile, the canyon forks. Go right and continue up the canyon. Look for brittlebush, beavertail cactus, buckhorn cholla, chuparosa, creosote, and desert lavender. After 0.4 mile, the trail climbs up and over a rock waterfall. After another 0.1 mile, the canyon gets very narrow and choked with vegetation. Return the way you came.

Maidenhair fern

BORREGO SPUR
(3.4 one way; Strenuous)

The easiest way to do this hike is to arrange a car shuttle, using two vehicles. The hike on the spur isn't very long, so you can also park at one end and return the way you came. If using two vehicles, leave one vehicle near the post office. (From The Circle, drive 0.2 mile west on Palm Canyon Drive and then turn left into The Mall and drive straight back to the parking area near the post office.) Then, return to Palm Canyon Drive. Turn left (west) and drive 1.1 miles to S22 (Montezuma Valley Road). Turn left onto S22 and drive south for 0.8 mile. Turn right (west) into the Hellhole Canyon parking area. Leave the second vehicle here. Remember to take the keys for the vehicle left at the post office.

Walk across S22 and then walk 0.1 mile east to the first toe of the ridge to the south. Follow the abandoned jeep road south as it climbs up the steep toe 0.6 mile to the top of the ridge. Walk another 0.4 mile west to the end of the road where there are good 360-degree views of Borrego Valley. Backtrack 0.1 mile and follow the trail to the northeast along the rocky ridge. Look for creosote, barrel cactus, and brittlebush on the hillsides. Walk 1.5 miles to the bottom of the ridge. Walk north 50 feet and turn right onto the jeep road. Walk 0.3 mile to Sunset Road and turn left. Walk 0.3 mile along Sunset Road in a northeasterly direction to the post office. Pick up the vehicle parked here earlier and return to the Hellhole Canyon parking area to pick up the second vehicle.

Gambel's quail

NOTES

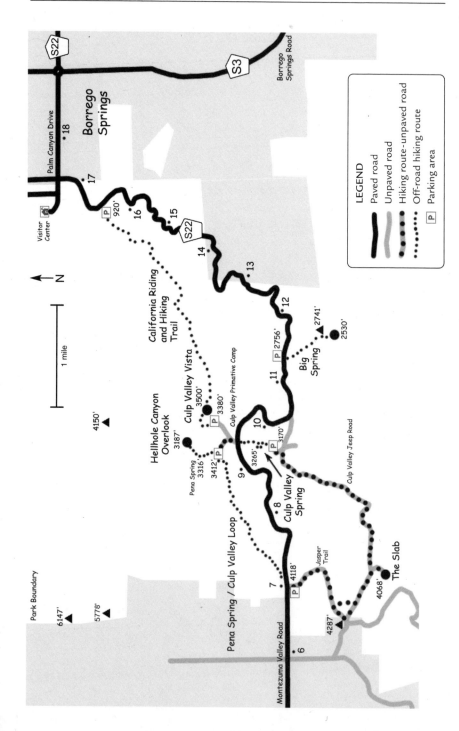

S22

S3

Borrego Springs Road

Borrego Springs

Palm Canyon Drive

• 18

17

Visitor Center

P 920'

16

15

S22

14

• 13

12

N

1 mile

California Riding and Hiking Trail

2741'

Big Spring

2530'

P 2756'

11

Culp Valley Vista 3500'

Hellhole Canyon Overlook 3187'

P 3380'

Culp Valley Primitive Camp

4150'

10

P 3170'

Pena Spring 3316'

P 3412'

3265'

Culp Valley Jeep Road

9

Culp Valley Spring

8

Pena Spring / Culp Valley Loop

Park Boundary

6147'

5778'

7

4118'

P

Jasper Trail

The Slab

4068'

4287'

Montezuma Valley Road

• 6

LEGEND

—— Paved road
—— Unpaved road
•—• Hiking route - unpaved road
••••• Off-road hiking route
P Parking area

AREA 6
CULP VALLEY

The higher elevation keeps Culp Valley somewhat cooler and wetter than the Borrego Valley. This is a transition zone, where plants from both the high and low desert grow.

BIG SPRING
(1.6 miles total; Moderate)

From The Circle in Borrego Springs, drive west on S22 (Palm Canyon Drive) for 1.3 miles. Turn left (south) onto S22 (Montezuma Valley Road). The parking area is at Mile 11.3 on S22 (approximately 5.9 miles up the grade). Park in the wide pullout on the right (north) side of the road.

Walk across S22 and follow the faint trail that goes toward the southeast for 0.2 mile. Look for cheesebush, desert mistletoe, buckhorn cholla, jojoba, lycium, yucca, catclaw, desert apricot, krameria, and brittlebush. Cross a low saddle and drop into a sandy wash. Look for agave, buckwheat, beavertail cactus, and sage. After 0.4 mile, stop at the top of the north fork of Tubb Canyon and enjoy the view. Backtrack 50 feet and go over the saddle to the south (left). Look for barrel cactus, mesquite, sugarbush, juniper, and hedgehog. Follow the faint trail for 0.2 mile to a dense thicket of cottonwood, willow, and catclaw. Near the north end of the thicket, water can be heard running from Big Spring. Backtrack to the top of the saddle. (Directly east is a rocky hill with superb views of Borrego Valley. A walk to the top of the hill will add 0.4 mile to the distance, and the difficulty rating will change to Strenuous.) Follow the trail toward the northeast (left) to return the way you came.

Scorpion

CULP VALLEY SPRING
(0.8 mile loop; Moderate)

From The Circle in Borrego Springs, drive west on S22 (Palm Canyon Drive) for 1.3 miles. Turn left (south) onto S22 (Montezuma Valley Road) and drive to Mile 10.5 (approximately 6.7 miles up the grade). Turn left (west) onto the Culp Valley jeep road. Drive west on this jeep road for 0.5 mile and then turn right (north) and drive 0.1 mile to a parking area.

There are large boulders at the north end of the parking area. Walk east and then north for 0.1 mile to get around these boulders, walking between this boulder hill and another farther to the east. Walk northwest toward the group of cottonwoods on the hill. These trees grow around a spring, which attracts birds and wildlife. Look for creosote, catclaw, desert mistletoe, sugarbush, buckhorn cholla, desert willow, sage, desert apricot, prickly pear, juniper, yucca, and buckwheat. After 0.1 mile, hike up the hillside by the best route possible, keeping the cottonwood trees on the left side. Walk counterclockwise around this spring and tangle of trees for 0.3 mile. Walk down the hill for 0.1 mile to complete the loop, and return the way you came for 0.2 mile to the parking area.

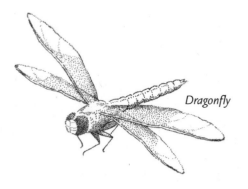

Dragonfly

PENA SPRING/CULP VALLEY LOOP

(8.8 mile loop; Strenuous)

From The Circle in Borrego Springs, drive west on S22 (Palm Canyon Drive) for 1.3 miles. Turn left (south) onto S22 (Montezuma Valley Road) and drive to Mile 9.2 (approximately 8.0 miles up the grade). There is a small sign on the right for Culp Valley Camp. Turn right (north) onto the jeep road. Drive 0.2 mile and then turn left. Drive 0.2 mile to the Pena Spring parking area at the end of the road.

Walk past the posts at the north end of the parking area. Walk north and then west 0.1 mile to the post for the California Riding & Hiking Trail. Turn left, and follow the steep trail up and around the rocky hill to the west for 1.0 mile. The walking is much easier for the rest of the hike. The next 2.0 miles goes through scrub made up of desert plum, catclaw, chemise, juniper, yucca, sage, cholla, and manzanita. In the springtime, it is possible to find many annuals not seen in the low desert. Cross S22 and walk west (uphill) along the edge of S22 approximately 20 feet to the Jasper Trail jeep road. Turn toward the south onto the jeep road and walk 0.5 mile, and then go right at the fork. Walk another 0.5 mile and turn left onto the California Riding & Hiking Trail. Look for sugarbush, scrub oak, juniper, and teddybear cholla. Walk 0.3 mile and then turn left onto the Culp Valley jeep road. Walk 3.0 miles down this road to reach Culp Valley. Turn left at the first fork and walk 0.1 mile north to a parking area. There are some large boulders at the north end of the parking area. Walk around the east side and then north side of these boulders for 0.1 mile, and then walk in a northwest direction for 0.5 mile toward the willow trees. Look for the trail on the east side of this spring and follow it toward the north for 0.5 mile to S22. Cross S22 and continue north to the jeep road (stay east of the hill). Follow the jeep road for 0.2 mile to the Pena Spring parking area.

Brittlebush

HELLHOLE CANYON OVERLOOK
(2.0 miles; Fairly Easy)

Follow the driving instruction for the Pena Spring/Culp Valley Loop hike (previous page).

Walk past the posts at the north end of the parking area and turn right into the small wash running down the hill. Look for sugarbush, buckhorn cholla, yucca, catclaw, and scrub oak. After 0.3 mile there will be an area with water seeping along the trail. The water is from Pena Spring to the west. The blackened shrubs are evidence of a wildfire that burned this area in 2002. Continue downhill in a northeast direction for 0.7 mile to a boulder outcrop that overlooks Hellhole Canyon. Look for desert willow, desert mistletoe, sage, krameria, and desert broom. There are views to the east of Borrego Valley and the Salton Sea beyond. Return the way you came.

CULP VALLEY VISTA
(1.0 mile total; Moderate)

From The Circle in Borrego Springs, drive west on S22 (Palm Canyon Drive) for 1.3 miles. Turn left (south) onto S22 (Montezuma Valley Road) and drive to Mile 9.2 (approximately 8.0 miles up the grade). There is a small sign on the right for Culp Valley Camp. Turn right (north) onto the jeep road. Drive 0.1 mile and go right at the fork. Continue another 0.1 mile to another fork. Continue straight (east) through the dry camp for 0.1 mile to the end of the road. Park near the sign for "Culp Valley Vista Point," which is the beginning of the hike.

Walk up the trail to the northeast for 0.2 mile. Look for sugarbush, buckhorn cholla, catclaw, desert mistletoe, juniper, yucca, scrub oak, krameria, and buckwheat. At the junction with the California Riding & Hiking Trail, turn right. Walk up the trail for 30 yards and turn right again. Walk another 0.3 mile to reach the vista point near the large boulders. There are good views of Culp Valley to the southwest, the Santa Rosa Mountains to the northeast, and Borrego Valley and Salton Sea to the east. Return the way you came.

CALIFORNIA RIDING & HIKING TRAIL

(6.2 one-way; Fairly Strenuous)

The easiest way to do this hike is to arrange a car shuttle, using two vehicles. From The Circle in Borrego Springs, drive west on S22 (Palm Canyon Drive) for 1.3 miles. Turn left onto S22 (Montezuma Valley Road) and drive south for 0.8 mile. Look for the information sign and turn right (west) into the Hellhole Canyon parking area. Park one vehicle near the information sign. Put all of the hikers and gear into the second vehicle. When you leave the Hellhole parking area, turn right and continue up S22 (Montezuma Valley Road) to Mile 9.2 (approximately 8.0 miles up the grade). There is a small sign on the right for Culp Valley Camp. Turn right (north) onto the jeep road. Drive 0.1 mile and go right at the fork. Continue another 0.1 mile to another fork. Continue straight (east) through the dry camp for 0.1 mile to the end of the road. Park near the sign for "Culp Valley Vista Point," which is the beginning of the hike. Remember to take the car keys for the vehicle left at the bottom.

Walk up the trail to the northeast for 0.2 mile. Look for sugarbush, buckhorn cholla, catclaw, desert mistletoe, juniper, yucca, scrub oak, krameria, and buckwheat. At the junction with the California Riding & Hiking Trail, turn right. Walk up the trail for 30 yards and turn right again. Walk another 0.3 mile to reach the vista point near the large boulders. There are good views of Culp Valley to the southwest, the Santa Rosa Mountains to the northeast, and Borrego Valley and Salton Sea to the east. Continue past the vista point and begin the 2,500-foot descent in altitude to the desert floor. After 0.4 mile, there will be another marker for CR&HT. Continue straight (east). Some sections of this trail are steep and covered with loose rocks. Culp Valley is a transitional zone, where juniper, manzanita, and sugar bush give way to ocotillo, agave, brittlebush, and creosote near the desert floor. After 4.0 miles of hiking from high to low desert, go left at the next CR&HT marker. Switchback down the hillside for 1.0 mile. At the bottom will be the trail to Hellhole Canyon. Turn right and follow the trail for 0.3 mile to the parking area. Pick up the vehicle parked here earlier and return to Culp Valley to pick up the second vehicle.

THE SLAB
(4.6 mile loop; Fairly Easy)

From The Circle in Borrego Springs, drive west on S22 (Palm Canyon Drive) for 1.3 miles. Turn left (south) onto S22 (Montezuma Valley Road) and drive to Mile 6.9 (approximately 10.3 miles up the grade). Turn left (south) onto the Jasper Ridge jeep road and park immediately on the right side of the jeep road. Parking is also available further up S22 on the wide shoulder at the top of the ridge.

Walk south on the Jasper Ridge jeep road for 0.5 mile. When the road forks, stay to the right and walk south on the jeep road for another 0.8 mile. Look for sugarbush, scrub oak, juniper, and teddybear cholla. At the intersection with the Culp Valley jeep road, turn left and walk east on the Culp Valley jeep road for 0.9 mile. Turn right (south) onto the jeep road that goes to The Slab. Follow this road south for 0.3 mile to the end. There used to be a slab for an old homestead in this area, but it was removed in the mid-1990s. Look for yucca and manzanita. Enjoy the views to the east of Culp Valley and Borrego Valley with the Salton Sea beyond. To return to the parking area, begin by backtracking 0.3 mile (north) to the Culp Valley jeep road. Turn left and walk west up the jeep road for 0.5 mile. Look for the sign on the right for the California Riding and Hiking Trail. Turn right (north) and follow the trail for 0.3 mile. When the CR&HT reaches the Jasper Ridge jeep road, turn to the right and walk on the jeep road toward the north for 1.0 mile to the parking area.

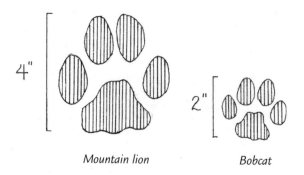

4"

2"

Mountain lion   Bobcat

NOTES

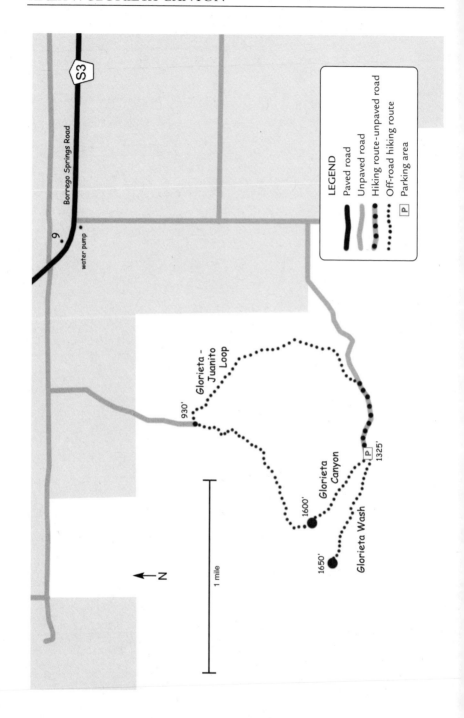

AREA 7
GLORIETA CANYON

Although it is close to Borrego Springs, Glorieta Canyon is not very well known. This area can be a good introduction to the variety of plants found in the desert. All of the hikes in this section begin at the same parking area.

The turnoff is at Mile 8.8 on Borrego Springs Road (approximately 3.2 miles south of The Circle). Just after the road turns to the east, turn right (south) onto the jeep road that is on the east side of the fenced water pump. Drive south for 1.3 miles. Where two jeep roads intersect, turn right and drive west for 1.4 miles. Park at the end of the road.

GLORIETA CANYON
(1.0 mile total; Moderate)

The trail begins at the west end of the parking area. Look for a trail that goes up the narrow, rocky canyon. Follow this trail as is winds up the canyon with low walls. Look for jojoba, catclaw, ocotillo, and barrel cactus. After 0.5 mile, the saddle will be reached. Return the way you came.

GLORIETA-JUANITO LOOP
(3.5 miles total; Strenuous)

Follow the walking instructions for the Glorieta Canyon hike until the saddle is reached. From the top of the saddle, a sandy wash is visible down to the right (north). Pick the best route available for the 0.2 hike down the short canyon to the rocky cairn next to the wash. Turn right and walk down the wash into Juanito Canyon. Pick the best route available through and around the areas with big boulders. After 0.5 mile, the mouth of the canyon and a sandy parking area will be reached. From the parking area, walk 0.1 mile toward the east and up onto the toe of the hill. Then head toward the southeast and south, through a beautiful forest of cholla cactus. Walk 1.7 miles to get around the mountain and to the jeep road you drove in on. Turn right and walk west on the jeep road for 0.6 mile to reach the vehicle. Drive back to the paved road the way you came.

GLORIETA WASH
(1.6 total; Fairly Easy)

Walk over the low berm to the south and into the wash (make a line of rocks in the sand to mark this spot). Turn right and walk up the wash in a westerly direction. This wash is mostly sandy with a few boulders. Look for ocotillo, jojoba, chuparosa, desert lavender, buckhorn cholla, catclaw, barrel cactus, brittlebush, indigo, teddybear cholla, and juniper. After 0.8 mile, the wash gets very rocky and then full of boulders. This is a good place to turn around. Return the way you came.

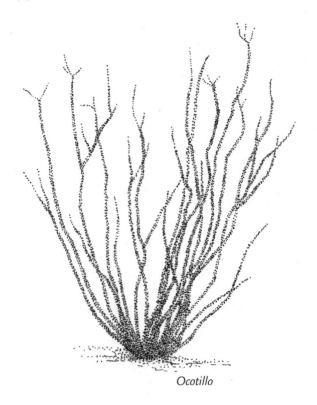

Ocotillo

NOTES

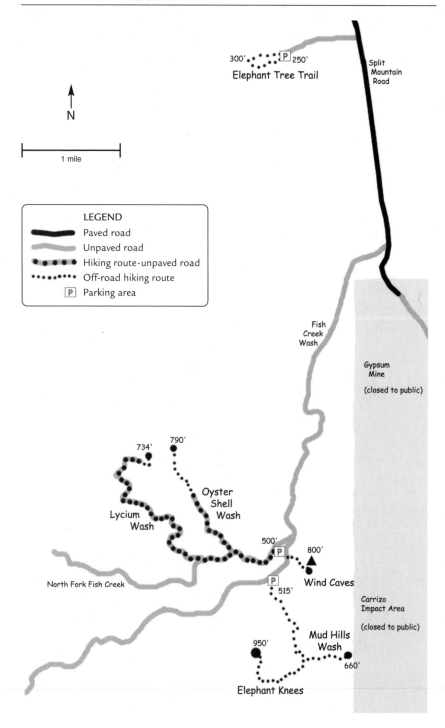

N

1 mile

LEGEND
Paved road
Unpaved road
Hiking route-unpaved road
Off-road hiking route
P   Parking area

300'   P 250'
Elephant Tree Trail

Split
Mountain
Road

Fish
Creek
Wash

Gypsum
Mine

(closed to public)

734'   790'

Oyster
Shell
Wash

Lycium
Wash

500'
P   800'
▲

North Fork Fish Creek   P   Wind Caves
515'

Carrizo
Impact Area

(closed to public)

950'   Mud Hills
Wash

660'

Elephant Knees

AREA 8
SPLIT MOUNTAIN

Split Mountain Gorge is an impressive sight, created by the down cutting of a stream as the mountains rose slowly through time. The desert willows and mesquite are evidence of underground water. To the south of Split Mountain lies the dry and desolate Fish Creek area, including the canyons and washes draining the Vallecito Mountains and Fish Creek Mountains.

ELEPHANT TREE TRAIL
(1.0 mile loop; Fairly Easy)

At the junction of Borrego Valley Road and Highway 78, drive east on Hwy 78 for approximately 6.4 miles. Turn right onto Split Mountain Road and drive south for approximately 5.6 miles. Look for the large information sign on the right. Turn right (west) onto the jeep road just before the sign. Drive west for 0.9 miles to the parking area at the end of the road.

The self-guided nature trail starts on the west side of the parking area. Look for the numbered posts along the route. Walk west and then southwest in the sandy wash at the base of the hill. The trail loops around the mouth of a wide wash in a clockwise direction. Look for cheesebush, brittlebush, indigo, catclaw, desert lavender, silver cholla, desert mistletoe, smoketree, buckhorn cholla, barrel cactus, creosote, and ocotillo. There is a magnificant elephant tree near trail marker #13, which is the halfway point in the loop trail. Continue the loop to return to the parking area.

Tarantula

MUD HILLS WASH
(5.2 miles total; Fairly Easy)

At the junction of Borrego Valley Road and Highway 78, drive east on Hwy 78 for approximately 6.4 miles. Turn right onto Split Mountain Road and drive south for approximately 7.7 miles. When the pavement ends, turn right onto the jeep road and drive southwest through Split Mountain, a wide canyon with very high sandstone walls. After 4.4 miles, park near the information sign on the low hill on the left side of the wash.

This hike follows the wash just to the east (left) of the information sign. If the ground is wet, this hike should be avoided because of mud. If the ground is dry, walk up the wash toward the south for 1.3 miles to the eastern edge of the first group of sandstone outcroppings called Elephant Knees. Look for saltbush, creosote, desert holly, buckwheat, thornbush, cheesebush, catclaw, and arrowweed. Continue to follow the wash for another 1.3 miles. Although the hills on either side of the wash are covered with mud, the rocks visible where large chunks of mud have fallen away reveal a fascinating geologic study. Be careful not to walk into the Carrizo Impact Area, which is closed to public entry. (There are no signs.) Return the way you came.

ELEPHANT KNEES
(3.6 miles total; Strenuous)

Follow the driving instructions for Mud Hills Wash.

This hike follows the wash just to the east (left) of the information sign. If the ground is wet, this hike should be avoided because of mud. If the ground is dry, walk up the wash toward the south for 1.3 miles to the eastern edge of the first group of sandstone outcroppings called Elephant Knees. Look for saltbush, creosote, desert holly, buckwheat, thornbush, cheesebush, catclaw, and arrowweed. Continue up the wash for another 0.1 mile to the base of a second set of Elephant Knees. Turn right (south) into Elephant Knees Wash and follow it toward the west. Look for small, fossilized oyster and scallop shells. (Warning: It is illegal to collect anything in the state park.) After 0.2 mile, the wash forks. Take the right fork and immediately turn right. Climb up the steep rocky hillside for 0.2 mile to the top of the butte. Don't get too close to the edge, but do enjoy the view of Split Mountain to the north and the mud hills to the southwest. Return the way you came.

WIND CAVES
(1.0 mile total; Strenuous)

At the junction of Borrego Valley Road and Highway 78, drive east on Hwy 78 for approximately 6.4 miles. Turn right onto Split Mountain Road and drive south for approximately 7.7 miles. When the pavement ends, turn right onto the jeep road and drive southwest through Split Mountain, a wide canyon with very high sandstone walls. Look for creosote, desert willow, cheesebush, smoketree, mesquite, desert mistletoe, and catclaw. After 3.9 miles, the canyon opens up. Drive another 0.2 mile and look for the trail to wind caves on the left. Park here on hard-packed sand, but do not block any of the jeep roads.

The well-worn trail begins by climbing up the hill to the east of the parking area. Look for the trail marker. The first part of the trail is steep and rocky. After 0.2 mile, go left at the fork. Look for ocotillo, creosote, saltbush, indigo, and barrel cactus. Another 0.3 mile will bring you to the caves. These are huge sandstone formations that have been eroded by wind and rain into imaginative shapes. After exploring the many formations, walk 0.1 mile to the top of the hill just to the west of the caves for wonderful views of the badlands to the west and Elephant Knees to the southwest. Return the way you came.

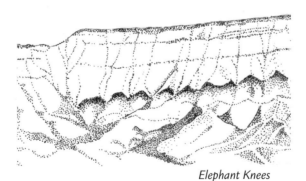

Elephant Knees

61

OYSTER SHELL WASH
(4.0 miles total; Fairly Strenuous)

At the junction of Borrego Valley Road and Highway 78, drive east on Hwy 78 for approximately 6.4 miles. Turn right onto Split Mountain Road and drive south for approximately 7.7 miles. When the pavement ends, turn right onto the jeep road and drive southwest through Split Mountain, a wide canyon with very high sandstone walls. After 3.9 miles, the canyon opens up. Drive another 0.2 mile and look for a jeep road going off to the west (right) and the trail to wind caves on the left. Park here on hard-packed sand, but do not block any of the jeep roads.

Walk along the jeep road that goes toward the west, which is signed for "North Fork Fish Creek." After 0.6 mile, turn right (north) onto the Oyster Shell Wash jeep road. Follow this road for 0.8 mile through mud hills to the end of the road. Look for mesquite, catclaw, creosote, smoketree, cheesebush, desert lavender, and desert mistletoe. Continue walking up the wash over several low, dry sandstone waterfalls. After 0.3 miles, a 15-foot-high dry waterfall is reached. Negotiate this waterfall and continue walking up the sandy wash for another 0.4 mile to a 30-foot-high dry waterfall. This is a good place to stop. Return the way you came.

LYCIUM WASH
(6.4 miles total; Fairly Easy)

Follow the driving instructions for Oyster Shell Wash.

Walk along the jeep road that goes toward the west, which is signed for "North Fork Fish Creek." After 0.9 mile, turn right (north) onto the Lycium Wash jeep road. Follow this road for 2.1 miles to the end of the road. Look for mesquite, catclaw, smoketree, creosote, ocotillo, desert lavender, and desert mistletoe. Continue walking up the wash for another 0.2 mile to a very narrow canyon. This is a good place to stop. Return the way you came.

AREA 9: BORREGO MOUNTAIN

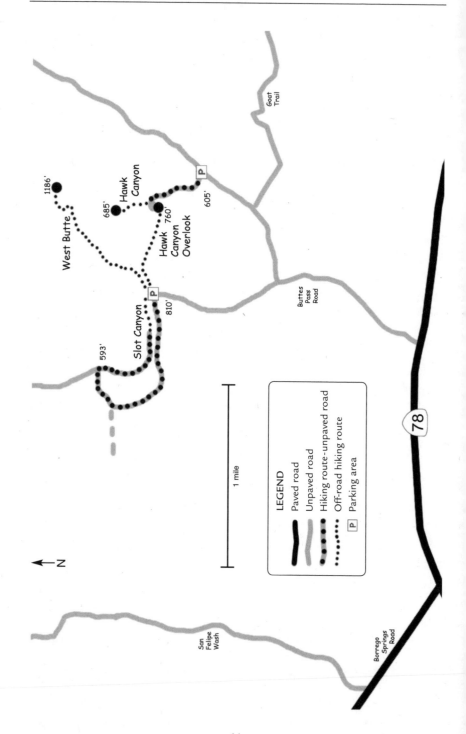

AREA 9
BORREGO MOUNTAIN

The western edge of Borrego Mountain is extremely eroded, and many slot canyons have formed in the sandstone. Only a few plants and animals have adapted to survive in this dry, sandy environment.

HAWK CANYON
(1.4 miles total; Moderate)

At the junction of Borrego Valley Road and Highway 78, drive east on Hwy 78 for 1.5 miles. Turn left (north) onto the Buttes Pass jeep road. After 0.9 mile, go right at the fork. After driving another 0.5 mile, go straight (left) at the fork. Drive 0.4 mile and park at the mouth of Hawk Canyon.

Walk west along the jeep road for 0.4 mile to the end of the road. Look for ironwood, creosote, smoketree, desert lavender, and brittlebush. Notice the color palette of greens, reds, yellows, and browns on the sides of the canyon indicating minerals in the soil. Hawks and falcons have been known to nest in this area. Continue walking northward into the canyon. After 0.3 mile, there is a 10-foot dry waterfall blocking the canyon. This is a good place to stop. Return the way you came.

HAWK CANYON OVERLOOK
(1.2 miles total; Fairly Strenuous)

At the junction of Borrego Valley Road and Highway 78, drive east on Hwy 78 for 1.5 miles. Turn left (north) onto the Buttes Pass jeep road. After 0.9 mile, go left (straight) at the fork. Drive north for another 0.8 mile and park on the north side of the jeep road junction, just before the road makes a sharp left.

Walk up the wash to the east for 0.2 mile. At the top of a ridge, turn right and walk 50 feet, and then turn left and follow the trail down the hill and along the ridge top. Look for creosote, ocotillo, and buckhorn cholla. After 0.4 mile, the trail will end at the edge of the hill. Hawk Canyon is directly below. Return the way you came.

WEST BUTTE

(2.2 miles total; Fairly Strenuous)

Follow the driving instructions for Hawk Canyon Overlook (previous page).

Walk east on the trail that goes along the south side of the canyon for 0.2 mile. Turn left and follow the trail along the ridge top for 0.5 mile. Look for creosote, ocotillo, brittlebush, krameria, and cholla. Just after climbing up a rocky part, the trail forks. Take the left fork and follow the trail up the side of the butte for 0.1 mile. When the trail forks again, take the right for a few steps and then look for a faint trail that goes off to the left, leading to the northeast. Follow this trail for 0.3 mile to the top of the butte. There is a sign-in book in a can at the top. Enjoy the panoramic views and then return the way you came.

Kangaroo rat tracks

SLOT CANYON
(2.0 mile loop; Moderate)

Follow the driving instructions for Hawk Canyon Overlook (previous page).

Walk west 0.9 mile on the jeep road that goes along the top of the ridge. There are good views of the Borrego Badlands to the north. Look for creosote, ocotillo, silver cholla, and saltbush. At the fork, continue straight for 0.1 mile to a parking area. Look for the sandy slide as the jeep road drops over the east edge of the ridge. Walk 0.2 mile down the slide and to the junction with the jeep road in the wash at the bottom. Wind and rain have eroded the sandstone hillsides into interesting formations. Turn right (south) and walk 0.5 mile to the end of the jeep road. Look for smoketree, brittlebush, alkali goldenbush, and desert holly. The wash continues toward the east and narrows into a wonderful slot canyon. After 0.2 mile, go right at the fork. Continue for another 0.1 mile and then begin to look for the trail on the right (south) side of the canyon. Scramble up this trail to the top, which is where the vehicle is parked. Note: The scramble up the canyon wall is easier farther up the drainage.

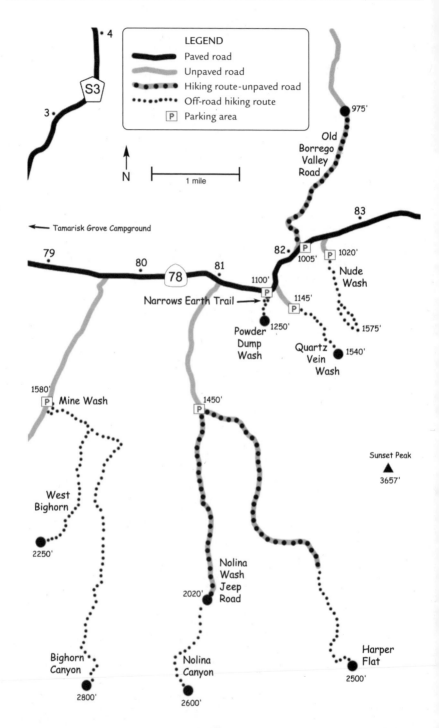

LEGEND

━━━ Paved road

━━━ Unpaved road

●●● Hiking route-unpaved road

•••• Off-road hiking route

P Parking area

N

1 mile

4

S3

3

← Tamarisk Grove Campground

Old Borrego Valley Road

975'

83

79

80

78

81

82

1005'

P 1020'

Nude Wash

1100'

Narrows Earth Trail →

P

1145'

P

1575'

Powder Dump Wash

1250'

Quartz Vein Wash

1540'

1580'

P Mine Wash

1450'

P

Sunset Peak

▲

3657'

West Bighorn

2250'

Nolina Wash Jeep Road

2020'

Bighorn Canyon

2800'

Nolina Canyon

2600'

Harper Flat

2500'

AREA 10
SUNSET MOUNTAIN

Sunset Mountain is a dominant feature in this section of the Vallecito Mountains. The washes and canyons that drain the Vallecitos and nearby Pinyon Mountains deserve your exploration.

NUDE WASH
(3.3 mile loop; Fairly Strenuous)

From the Tamarisk Grove intersection, drive east on Highway 78 for 5.5 miles. Turn right (south) onto a jeep road and drive 0.3 mile to the end of the road.

Walk south up the wash for 0.1 mile. Bypass the first dry waterfall on the left side. Continue walking up the canyon and look for ironwood, creosote, ocotillo, barrel cactus, agave, catclaw, brittlebush, and chuparosa. The rest of the canyon is a series of dry waterfalls from 2-to-20-feet high with sections of sand and boulders between them. Look for jojoba, ephedra, pencil cholla, buckhorn cholla, desert lavender, and teddybear cholla. After 0.6 mile, take the left fork. Walk for another 0.2 mile to where the canyon forks into two drainages filled with rocks and vegetation. This is where the loop begins and ends. Walk up the drainage on the left for 0.1 mile to a small bowl. Walk straight across this flat area and then up toward the east for 0.5 mile to the top of the drainage. Look for krameria and indigo. Walk 0.1 mile to the saddle on the right and then down into the drainage to the south. Walk down this drainage for 0.8 mile to return to Nude Wash and where the loop began. Turn left and walk down the canyon 0.9 mile to return to the parking area.

Lark sparrow

OLD BORREGO VALLEY ROAD
(3.4 miles total; Moderate)

From the Tamarisk Grove intersection, drive east on Highway 78 for 5.4 miles and park on the right (south) side of Highway 78, near the transformer station.

Walk west on Highway 78 for 50 feet (be careful if there is traffic) and cross the highway to the beginning of the Old Borrego Valley Road. Walk north on the jeep road. Look for smoketree, agave, creosote, buckhorn cholla, saltbush, ocotillo, barrel cactus, brittlebush, catclaw, jojoba, ephedra, indigo, and a large forest of teddybear cholla. The road forks after 0.4 mile. Continue straight (east) and follow the jeep road for another 1.3 mile, to the top of a rise. Enjoy the views of Borrego Mountain to the east, Santa Rosa Mountains and Borrego Valley to the north, San Ysidro Mountains to the west, and Vallecito Mountains to the south. Do not continue north on the jeep road as it soon enters private property. Return the way you came.

QUARTZ VEIN WASH
(1.8 miles total; Fairly Strenuous)

From the Tamarisk Grove intersection, drive east on Highway 78 for 4.7 miles. Turn right (south) onto the jeep road for Quartz Vein Wash and drive 0.4 mile to the end of the jeep road. Look for the many ironwood trees in this wash. Park near the end of the jeep road.

Walk up the fork on the left side and over the low dry waterfall. Follow the wash for 0.3 mile to some large boulders, which can be negotiated on the left side. Look for chuparosa, catclaw, desert lavender, creosote, agave, ocotillo, barrel cactus, and teddybear cholla. Continue up the wash, which has several dry waterfalls to be negotiated. Look for brittlebush, jojoaba, and ephedra. After 0.5 mile, the wash forks. Take the left fork and continue for 0.1 mile to a 15-foot-high waterfall. This is a good place to stop. Return the way you came.

Beetle tracks

NARROWS EARTH TRAIL
(0.3 mile loop; Fairly Easy)

From the Tamarisk Grove intersection, drive east on Highway 78 for 4.5 miles. Parking is available at the wide pullouts on either side of the road. The trailhead is on the south side of Highway 78.

The trail begins at the east end of the parking area. Look for the marker on a post. The trail loops around the mouth of the canyon. Several earthquake faults run through this area, and the hillsides on either side are made of rocks folded and twisted by past seismic activity. Look for indigo, agave, catclaw, ocotillo, creosote, buckhorn cholla, chuparosa, and brittlebush.

POWDER DUMP WASH
(0.8 mile total; Moderate)

Follow the driving instructions for Narrows Earth Trail.

A trail begins at the east end of the parking area for Narrows Earth Trail. Look for the marker on a post. Follow this trail toward the south for 0.2 mile to the narrow opening of the canyon. Look for catclaw, buckhorn cholla, creosote, ocotillo, indigo, brittlebush, and chuparosa. Walk up the canyon for 0.2 mile to a 10-foot-high dry waterfall. This is a good place to stop. Look for jojoba and agave. Return the way you came.

NOLINA WASH JEEP ROAD
(4.0 miles total; Fairly Easy)

From the Tamarisk Grove intersection, drive east on Highway 78 for 3.9 miles. Turn right (south) onto the jeep road for Pinyon Wash and drive south for 1.6 miles. Look for smoketree, creosote, agave, desert lavender, ironwood, buckhorn cholla, and rabbit brush. Park on hard-packed sand near where the jeep road forks, but do not block any of the jeep roads.

Walk up the right fork toward the south. Follow the jeep road as it goes up a wide sandy wash between hills covered with boulders, ocotillo, teddybear cholla, and agave. Look for the plants listed in the driving instructions as well as jojoba, catclaw, chuparosa, ephedra, desert willow, and desert mistletoe. The jeep road ends after 2.0 miles. Return the way you came.

NOLINA CANYON
(3.4 miles total; Moderate)

Follow the driving instructions for Nolina Wash Jeep Road (previous page).

Follow the hiking instructions for Nolina Wash Jeep Road (previous page). At the end of the jeep road, walk around the large boulder and continue up the sandy wash for 1.4 miles. Look for the plants listed for the Nolina Wash Jeep Road hike as well as juniper, barrel cactus, brittlebush, desert apricot, yucca, and climbing milkweed. When the wash narrows to a canyon, walk up the 3-foot-high dry waterfall and continue up the canyon for another 0.1 mile to where the canyon forks. Take the left fork and walk up the dry waterfall. Continue up the canyon for 0.2 mile. The canyon ends at a 50-foot-high dry waterfall. Return the way you came.

HARPER FLAT
(7.8 miles total; Fairly Strenuous)

Follow the driving instructions for Nolina Wash Jeep Road (previous page).

Walk up the left fork toward the southeast and then south. Follow the jeep road for 3.3 miles. Look for desert lavender, smoketree, catclaw, ocotillo, chuparosa, brittlebush, buckhorn cholla, teddybear cholla, desert willow, agave, desert mistletoe, rabbit brush, ephedra, jojoba, and creosote. There is a wall of large boulders at the end of the jeep road. Follow the trail to the right side as it winds around and over the boulders for 0.1 mile. Continue up the sandy wash for another 0.5 mile to the edge of Harper Flat. Look for desert apricot, juniper, and indigo. Explore the area, and then return the way you came.

Desert willow flower

BIGHORN CANYON
(8.4 miles total; Fairly Strenuous)

From the Tamarisk Grove intersection, drive east on Highway 78 for 2.7 miles. Turn right (south) onto the jeep road for Mine Wash, and drive toward the south for 1.5 miles. Look for smoketree, cholla, and indigo. The wide parking area is near an information sign and several ironwood trees.

Walk toward the east, keeping the boulder-covered hill to your right, and then continue southeast in the sandy wash. Look for fishhook cactus, hedgehog cactus, cholla, beavertail, agave, ocotillo, creosote, indigo, jojoba, and catclaw. After 0.8 mile, two canyons are visible to the south. Bighorn Canyon is the canyon farthest to the east. Leave the wash and walk 0.6 mile to the mouth of Bighorn Canyon, and then head south into the canyon. Look for desert lavender, ephedra, cheesebush, barrel cactus, mesquite, desert mistletoe, desert willow, desert apricot, juniper, and sage. After 2.3 miles, go right at the fork. Walk for 0.3 mile to a series of sheep tanks, which are used to provide water for bighorn sheep and other wildlife. Look for yucca. Continue up the canyon for another 0.2 mile to an 8-foot-high dry waterfall. This is a good place to stop. Return the way you came.

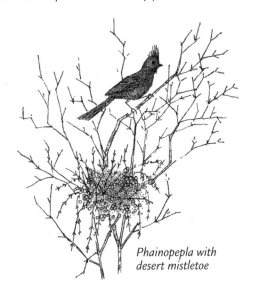

*Phainopepla with
desert mistletoe*

WEST BIGHORN
(4.8 miles total; Fairly Strenuous)

Follow the driving instructions for Bighorn Canyon.

Walk toward the east, keeping the boulder-covered hill to your right, and then continue southeast in the sandy wash. Look for fishhook cactus, hedgehog cactus, cholla, beavertail, agave, ocotillo, creosote, indigo, jojoba, and catclaw. After 0.8 mile, two canyons are visible to the south. West Bighorn is the canyon to the west. Continue walking in the wash and then into the canyon. Look for juniper. After 1.6 miles, there is a saddle. This is a good place to stop. Mine Wash is visible to the west. Enjoy the views, and then return the way you came.

MINE WASH

(0.2 mile total; Fairly Easy)

From the Tamarisk Grove intersection, drive east on Highway 78 for 2.7 miles. Turn right (south) onto the jeep road for Mine Wash, and drive toward the south for 1.5 miles. Look for smoketree, cholla, and indigo. The wide parking area is near an information sign and several ironwood trees.

Walk toward the east and explore the boulders and natural rock shelters. This Kumeyaay village site was occupied as early as twelve hundred years ago, and many morteros (grinding holes) and metates (grinding slicks) are visible on the rocks.

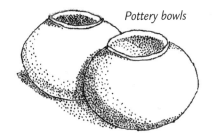

Pottery bowls

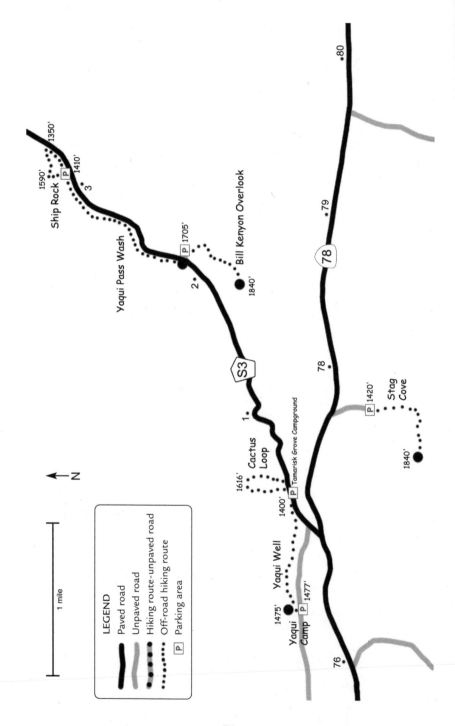

AREA 11
TAMARISK GROVE

Tamarisk Grove is a popular campground in Anza-Borrego Desert State Park. In some years, during winter months, the tamarisk trees that shade each campsite provide roosts for long-eared owls. Bighorn sheep can occasionally be seen on Pinyon Ridge, the rocky hills to the north of the campground. Nearby is Yaqui Well, a natural spring that provides a year-round source of water for birds and other wildlife. South of Tamarisk Grove Campground are many accessible side canyons draining the Vallecito Mountains, including Quartz Vein Wash and Narrows Earth Trail, all well worth exploring (See Area 10).

SHIP ROCK
(0.7 mile loop; Strenuous)

The parking area is at Mile 3.1 on S3 (Yaqui Pass Road), approximately 3.1 miles north of the Tamarisk Grove intersection. There is a wide sandy area at the bottom of Yaqui Pass Wash, on the left (west) side of S3, with enough room for several vehicles. Park here.

The hill on the northwest side of the parking area is Ship Rock. There is no trail, so choose the best route available, climbing in a northwest direction. Look for cholla, creosote, brittlebush, and barrel cactus. The top is reached after a 0.2 mile climb. There are excellent views of the Borrego Valley to the north and the Salton Sea to the east. There are two survey markers on top and a can with a sign-in book. To descend, choose the best route available, walking down in a north-by-northeast direction. After 0.3 mile, the sandy wash that parallels S2 will be reached. Turn to the right and walk up the wash, toward the south. Look for smoketree, ocotillo, desert lavender, chuparosa, and jojoba. The parking area is reached after 0.2 mile.

Coyote melon

YAQUI PASS WASH
(2.0 miles total; Fairly Easy)

The parking area is at Mile 3.1 on S3 (Yaqui Pass Road), approximately 3.1 miles north of the Tamarisk Grove intersection. There is a wide sandy area at the bottom of Yaqui Pass Wash, on the left (west) side of S3, with enough room for several vehicles. Park here.

Walk up the sandy wash in a southerly direction as it parallels Yaqui Pass Road. Plants in this wash include jojoba, chuparosa, creosote, indigo, smoketree, and desert lavender. After 1.0 mile, the wash will be almost level with the road. Across the road is the entrance to Yaqui Camp and near to the beginning of the Bill Kenyon Overlook hike. Return the way you came.

BILL KENYON OVERLOOK
(1.0 mile total; Moderate)

The parking area is at Mile 2.1 on S3 (Yaqui Pass Road), approximately 2.1 miles north of the Tamarisk Grove intersection. Turn right (east) at the marker for Yaqui Camp. This is a popular dry camping area. Drive in to the right for 0.1 mile and park near the trailhead sign.

The trail leads south and then crosses over a rocky hillside. Look for creosote, indigo, ocotillo, agave, brittlebush, saltbush, buckhorn cholla, jojoba, teddybear cholla, krameria, desert lavender, and barrel cactus. After 0.5 mile, turn left and walk 50 feet to the information sign for Mescal Bajada. You will see Highway 78 and San Felipe Wash below and the Pinyon Mountains beyond. Return the way you came.

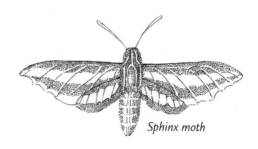

Sphinx moth

CACTUS LOOP
(1.1 mile loop; Strenuous)

The parking area is at Mile 0.4 on S3, (Yaqui Pass Road), approximately 0.4 mile north of the Tamarisk Grove intersection. Park along the fence on the south (right) side of the road near the entrance to Tamarisk Grove Campground.

Cross the road and walk to where the trail begins, directly across from the entrance to the campground. The trail begins by following the west side of a rocky wash, and then it crosses the wash and climbs up through a large patch of ocotillo. When you reach the top, turn right and walk 100 feet to a lookout point. Backtrack to the main trail and turn right to continue the loop. The trail now descends a rocky hillside. There are many brittlebush and barrel cactus on this side of the hill, as well as ocotillo and teddybear cholla. When you reach Yaqui Pass Road, turn right and walk 200 feet to where you started.

YAQUI WELL
(1.6 miles total; Moderate)

Follow the driving instructions for Cactus Loop.

Walk west on the road 0.1 mile and cross the road. The trail starts on the north side of the road, just west of the park's employee residence. The first part of the trail goes up and over a low rocky hill. Look for fishhook cactus, thornbush, cholla, ocotillo, brittlebush, and creosote. Once the trail drops down off of the hill, it becomes sandy and is lined with rocks. Look for ironwood trees covered with desert mistletoe and the distinctly crested phainopeplas that feed on the mistletoe berries. Walk through a mesquite forest to Yaqui Well, a seep used by birds and other animals as a permanent water source. This is a good place to sit quietly and observe desert wildlife. Return the way you came.

YAQUI CAMP
(0.2 mile total; Fairly Easy)

From the Tamarisk Grove intersection, drive northeast on S3 (Yaqui Pass Road) for 0.1 mile and turn left (west) onto the jeep road for Yaqui Well Camp. Drive west for 0.5 mile and the turn right into the parking area.

Begin walking near the information sign and follow the trail for 0.1 mile to Yaqui Well. Look for ironwood, creosote, saltbush, mesquite, thornbush, and desert mistletoe. Yaqui Well is a permanent source of water for wildlife and a good place for birding, especially during spring and fall migration. Return the way you came.

STAG COVE
(1.6 miles total; Moderate)

From the Tamarisk Grove intersection, drive east on Highway 78 for 0.8 mile. Turn right (south) onto the jeep road for Stag Cove. Drive south for 0.2 mile and park at the end of the road.

Walk up the sandy canyon toward the south. Look for ocotillo, catclaw, indigo, cholla, desert lavender, creosote, jojoba, agave, and chuparosa. After 0.2 mile, the canyon becomes slightly narrower and there are more boulders. After another 0.3 mile, there is debris in the bottom of the canyon from a rockslide, which can be bypassed on the left side. After another 0.1 mile, go right at the fork. Continue for another 0.2 mile and then stop when negotiating the boulders makes walking more difficult. Return the way you came.

Jackrabbit tracks

NOTES

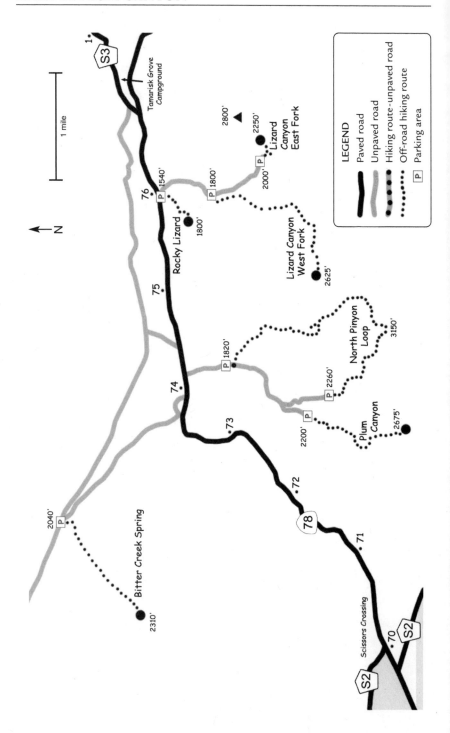

LEGEND
- Paved road
- Unpaved road
- Hiking route – unpaved road
- Off-road hiking route
- P Parking area

N

1 mile

S3
1

Tamarisk Grove Campground

2800'
2250'
Lizard Canyon East Fork
2000'
1800'
1540'
76
Rocky Lizard
1800'
75
Lizard Canyon West Fork
2625'

North Pinyon Loop
3150'
1820'
2260'
2200'
Plum Canyon
2675'
74
73
72
78
71

2040'
Bitter Creek Spring
2310'

Scissors Crossing
70
S2
S2
S2

Area 12
Plum Canyon

The Pinyon Mountains have several interesting canyons on the north side. These rugged canyons vary in their geology and vegetation. Just to the north of these canyons, in the Yaqui Flat and Grapevine Canyon areas, cattle were grazed in the early 1900s.

LIZARD CANYON – EAST FORK
(0.8 mile total; Fairly Strenuous)

From the Tamarisk Grove intersection, drive west on Highway 78 for 0.9 mile. Turn left (south) onto the jeep road and drive southeast for 1.5 miles to the end of the road. Look for cholla, barrel cactus, hedgehog cactus, agave, ocotillo, catclaw, chuparosa, cheesebush, brittlebush, desert lavender, indigo, juniper, and desert apricot.

Walk south into the canyon for 0.1 mile. The canyon forks near a large juniper tree. The main drainage is up the right fork, where the canyon walls are white granite. A 0.1-mile walk ends at the bottom of a dry waterfall. Backtrack 0.1 mile to the juniper tree and walk up the left fork, toward the east. Look for desert apricot, brittlebush, jojoba, ephedra, agave, cholla, hedgehog cactus, fishhook cactus, barrel cactus, and juniper. After 0.2 mile, there will be a large boulder on the left and a large juniper tree on the right. This is a good place to stop. Walk back down the canyon to return to the vehicle.

3·15-08   w/ CHARLIE

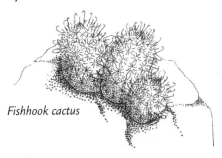

Fishhook cactus

LIZARD CANYON-WEST FORK
(4.8 miles total; Fairly Strenuous)

From the Tamarisk Grove intersection, drive west on Highway 78 for 0.9 mile. Turn left (south) onto the jeep road and drive toward the southeast for 0.8 mile. Park at the mouth of the wide wash on the right (west) side of the jeep road.

Walk into the wash and follow it toward the south. Look for chuparosa, brittlebush, desert lavender, ocotillo, creosote, catclaw, barrel cactus, cholla, beavertail cactus, agave, ephedra, indigo, and jojoba. After 0.5 mile, go right at the fork and continue to follow the main drainage for another 1.2 miles. Look for juniper and desert apricot. Go right at the next fork, walk 0.2 mile, go right at another fork, walk 0.3 mile, go left at the next fork, and walk 0.2 mile up the drainage to the top of a saddle. Look for fishhook cactus and hedgehog cactus. Enjoy the views of Pinyon Ridge to the North, the Vallecito Mountains to the east, and the Lagunas in the distance to the southwest. Return the way you came.

ROCKY LIZARD
(1.4 miles total; Fairly Strenuous)

From the Tamarisk Grove intersection, drive west on Highway 78 for 0.9 mile. Turn left (south) onto the jeep road and park next to the paved road.

Walk south into the canyon. Look for creosote, chuparosa, catclaw, ocotillo, agave, and desert lavender. The next 0.6 mile is rockier and steeper. Look for jojoba and brittlebush. Choose the easiest route available up to the saddle, which has interesting views into the wash on the other side. Return the way you came.

Stinkbug

NORTH PINYON LOOP
(4.2 miles total; Strenuous)

This hike is best done using two vehicles. From the Tamarisk Grove intersection, drive west on Highway 78 for 2.7 miles. Turn left (south) onto the jeep road for Plum Canyon. Drive south for 0.5 mile and park one vehicle. Put all hikers and gear into the second vehicle and continue driving south for another 0.8 mile, and then go left at the fork. Drive 0.5 mile to the end of the road and park.

Walk south into the canyon for 0.2 mile to a dry waterfall, which can be negotiated on the right side. Look for teddybear cholla, chuparosa, brittlebush, catclaw, ephedra, juniper, agave, ocotillo, creosote, desert apricot, barrel cactus, lycium, beavertail cactus, sage, buckhorn cholla, buckwheat, and hedgehog cactus. Continue walking for another 0.3 mile and go left at the fork. Walk another 0.5 mile to where the canyon forks at two dry waterfalls. Take the left fork and negotiate the 30-foot-high dry waterfall. Continue up the drainage toward the east for another 0.4 mile. At the top of the drainage, walk east for 0.1 mile through the low saddle and then northeast 0.1 mile to the edge of a deep canyon. Do not descend here. Instead, turn left (north) and walk down the hill for 0.2 mile. Then, turn right and walk down the drainage for 0.3 mile toward the east and the bottom of the deep canyon. At the bottom, turn left (north) and walk down the main canyon for 0.5 mile to the top of a 50-foot-high dry waterfall. Do not attempt this waterfall. Instead, walk back up the canyon 100 feet and look for the best route up the low ridge on the right (west) side of the main canyon. Climb up, over, and down this ridge for 0.3 mile to reach the bottom of the drainage to the west. At the bottom, turn right and walk down this drainage toward the north for 0.3 mile to reach the main canyon. Follow the main canyon downhill and toward the north for 0.6 mile to the mouth of the canyon. Continue walking down the wash for another 0.2 mile and then turn left, climb out of the wash, and walk toward the west. After 0.2 mile, the jeep road for Plum Canyon will be reached, and the first vehicle should be nearby.

PLUM CANYON
(3.5 miles total; Fairly Strenuous)

From the Tamarisk Grove intersection, drive west on Highway 78 for 2.7 miles. Turn left (south) onto the jeep road for Plum Canyon. Drive south for 1.3 miles and go right at the fork. Drive another 0.4 mile and park at the end of the road.

Walk south up the sandy wash. This hike follows the California Riding and Hiking Trail most of the way. Look for the small succulent called live forever (or dudlyea) tucked into the rock crevices. After 0.2 mile, look for the CR&HT marker and go right to bypass the big boulders. Continue walking south for 100 feet and then go right at the fork. After another 0.5 mile, look for the CR&HT marker and go left at the fork. Despite the canyon's name, no desert plum is found here, but do look for mesquite, creosote, yucca, desert lavender, sage, ocotillo, catclaw, ephedra, desert mistletoe, desert apricot, barrel cactus, hedgehog cactus, teddybear cholla, buckhorn cholla, beavertail cactus, prickly pear cactus, juniper, desert fir, and saltbush. Walk 0.2 mile to another CR&HT marker and go right at this point to get around the rocky section. Continue up the wash (on a rocky trail where the incline is a bit steeper) for 0.6 mile to reach a saddle overlooking the small community of Shelter Valley. Walk another 0.1 mile for a better view. Return the way you came.

Yucca

BITTER CREEK SPRING
(3.0 miles total; Fairly Easy)

From the Tamarisk Grove intersection, drive west on Highway 78 for 2.6 miles. Turn right (north) onto the jeep road for Grapevine Canyon. Drive for 2.0 miles to an open area where two jeep roads join and there is a park road marker. Park here.

Look toward the southwest. You are standing in the mouth of a wide valley that tapers toward the back. Follow the sandy wash at the base of the hill on the left (south) side of the valley's mouth for 1.0 mile. Look for creosote, ocotillo, saltbush, indigo, desert willow, catclaw, smoketree, juniper, ephedra, jojoba, krameria, desert apricot, yucca, agave, buckhorn cholla, teddybear cholla, barrel cactus, hedgehog cactus, and prickly pear cactus. When the valley narrows, walk 0.2 mile and then take the left fork. Walk another 0.2 mile and take the left fork. Walk 0.1 mile and look for the clump of creosote and yucca on the left side of the canyon. Behind the creosote is an old bathtub with pipes running up the hillside. The cottonwood tree high on the hill indicates the location of the spring that was used to fill the bathtub when cattle roamed this area in the early 1900s. Return the way you came.

*Costa's hummingbird
with ocotillo flower*

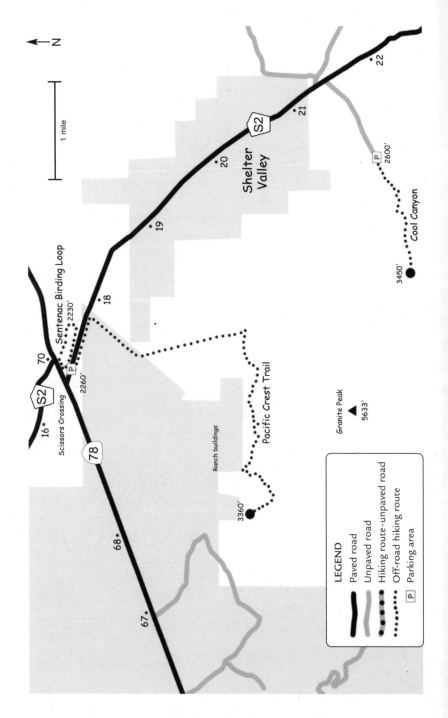

AREA 13
SHELTER VALLEY

This section is just south of Scissors Crossing, the local name for the junction of County Road S2 and State Highway 78. The hikes in this area are near the small community of Shelter Valley, formerly known as Earthquake Valley. This area is slightly higher and receives more rainfall than the Borrego Valley.

SENTENAC BIRDING LOOP
(1.2 mile loop; Fairly Easy)

From Scissors Crossing, drive 0.2 mile south on S2. Parking is available on either side of the road just past the sign for the Pacific Crest Trail (PCT).

Look for the well-worn trail on the east side of S2 between the fence posts. Follow this trail past the yellow boundary marker for the state park and the wooden post for the PCT. Continue on this part of the PCT toward the northeast for 0.2 mile as the trail drops down a low hill, parallels Highway 78, passes through an old stock gate (which should be left closed), and then crosses San Felipe Creek. Look for catclaw, mesquite, creosote, saltbush, buckhorn cholla, seep willow, and cottonwood trees. Just after crossing the creek, look for an opening in the fence on the right. Walk through this opening and follow the trail, which is marked with 3-foot-high wooden posts, as it winds toward the south for 0.4 mile. The trail then turns toward the east and then northeast. Some of the trees and shrubs have blackened trunks, evidence of a wildfire that burned through this area several years ago. Look for yucca, thornbush, and alkali goldenbush. After 0.5 mile, there will be a fence with an opening in it. Walk through this opening and then another 20 feet to the PCT. Turn left and walk up the low hill and another 0.1 mile to the parking area. This riparian area is a good place to look for birds at any time of year, particularly during spring and fall migration.

PACIFIC CREST TRAIL
(9.8 miles total; Fairly Strenuous)

Follow the driving instructions for Sentenac Birding Loop (previous page).

The trail begins on the west side of S2 at the gate in the fence. (The first part of this trail crosses private land, so please stay on the trail and leave all gates closed.) Walk through the gate and turn left (south) and walk on the worn path for 0.6 mile along the fence. The trail then turns toward the southwest and goes along another fence for 0.4 mile to another gate. Go through the gate and continue on the trail toward the southeast for 1.4 miles. Look for catclaw, ephedra, creosote, buckhorn cholla, juniper, buckwheat, yucca, agave, hedgehog cactus, desert apricot, and jojoba. The trail now turns toward the west along the base of Granite Mountain. Follow the trail for another 2.5 miles to the top of the ridge overlooking the top end of Rodriguez Canyon. Look for sugarbush, sage, chemise, prickly pear cactus, and scrub oak. There are several old gold mines across the valley. Banner Grade, which leads up to Julian, is visible to the west. Enjoy the view. Return the way you came.

COOL CANYON
(5.0 miles total; Strenuous)

The turnoff to Cool Canyon is at Mile 21.4 on S2 (approximately 4.3 miles south of Scissors Crossing). Just south of the large wooden sign for the state park, turn right (west) onto a jeep road (no sign) and drive for 1.0 mile. Park at the end of the road.

The trail heads west into the canyon. The trail is mostly sandy with some rocky dry waterfalls. The canyon has steep rocky walls with lots of agave, yucca, barrel cactus, juniper, and desert apricot. Walk 1.2 miles, then scramble up a 30-foot-high dry waterfall, and then a 12-foot-high dry waterfall just beyond that. The vegetation now gets thicker and the terrain rockier. After another 1.0 mile, the brush gets very thick. Look for the rock cairn visible on a hillside to the left. This is a good place to stop. Return the way you came.

NOTES

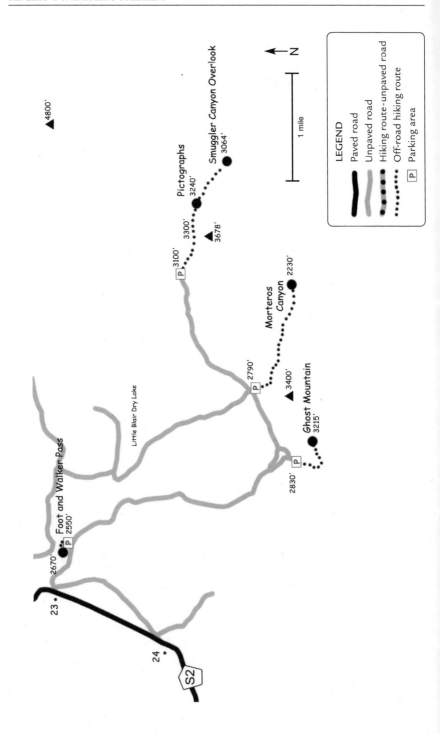

AREA 14
BLAIR VALLEY

Blair Valley is a popular area for dry camping in the winter. There is a long history of people living in this area, and the evidence is visible along some of these hikes.

FOOT & WALKER PASS
(0.7 mile total; Strenuous)

The Blair Valley turnoff is on the east side of S2 at Mile 22.9 (look for the sign approximately 5.7 miles south of Scissors Crossing). Drive east and then south along the base of the hills on the jeep road for 0.5 mile. Turn left at the small arrow for a California historical monument and drive northeast for 0.1 mile to the parking area.

Stand next to the vehicle and look at the small hill to the north. Try to find the historical monument near the top. This will be the first stop. To reach the monument, walk north and then go left at the fork. Walk 50 feet up a steep and rocky trail (the original Butterfield Overland Stage route), turn to the right, and follow the rocky steps up to the monument. The monument is 0.1 mile from the parking area. Backtrack to the Butterfield Overland Stage route, turn right, and continue in a northwestern direction up to the pass. Look for creosote, krameria, yucca, buckhorn cholla, and ephedra. From the top of the pass, turn left (west), and follow the trail 0.2 mile to the top of the hill for good views of Blair Valley to the southwest and Little Blair Valley to the northeast. Look for agave, ocotillo, catclaw, prickly pear cactus, jojoba, and desert mistletoe. Return to the vehicle by walking back down to the stage route and following it down to the parking area.

California historical monument

GHOST MOUNTAIN

(~~1.6~~ **2.0** miles total; Strenuous)

The Blair Valley turnoff is on the east side of S2 at Mile 22.9 (look for the sign approximately 5.7 miles south of Scissors Crossing). Drive east and then south along the base of the hills on the jeep road that goes through the valley. This area has lots of agave, yucca, ocotillo, juniper, and cholla. After 1.2 miles, look for an arrow on a post directing vehicles to go right. Drive another 1.7 miles to a fork and turn right. Drive for 0.3 mile and turn right again. Drive 0.1 mile to the parking area at the end of the road.

The trail is a steep climb up a rocky slope to the Marshal South homesite. The South family lived on the mountain for sixteen years during the 1930s and 1940s and carried everything, including water, up to the homesite. Remnants of the homestead still stand at the top of the mountain. The views are fantastic. The trail begins on the south side of the parking area near the information sign. The first 0.5 mile switchbacks up a steep and rocky hillside. Look for agave, juniper, yucca, ephedra, prickly pear, buckhorn cholla, jojoba, krameria, hedgehog cactus, and barrel cactus. The trail then levels out for 0.1 mile. The Carrizo Badlands are to the south, and Blair Valley is to the north. The next 0.1 mile climbs up the rocky hillside. The trail then levels out for the next 0.1 mile to the remains of the homesite. When you leave the site, head directly west to return the way you came.

3·19·08   W/ CHARLIE

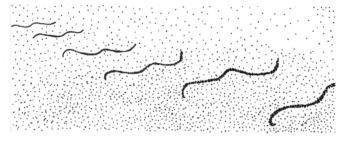

Sidewinder tracks

MORTEROS CANYON
(2.8 miles total; Strenuous)

The Blair Valley turnoff is on the east side of S2 at Mile 22.9 (look for the sign approximately 5.7 miles south of Scissors Crossing). Drive east and then south along the base of the hills on the jeep road that goes through the valley. This area has lots of agave, yucca, ocotillo, juniper, and cholla. After 1.2 miles, look for an arrow on a post directing vehicles to go right. Drive another 1.7 miles to a fork and turn left (east). Drive 0.2 mile and turn left again. Drive 0.5 mile to the parking area on the right (south) side of the road.

Walk south along the well-used trail for 0.2 mile to an area with large boulders. This was the site of a Kumeyaay village. There are many morteros (grinding holes) and metates (slick areas on rock surfaces) that were used to prepare food. Stay to the left (east) side of the canyon and continue walking down the canyon toward the south. Several places require careful boulder scrambling. Look for barrel cactus, beavertail, desert lavender, catclaw, desert apricot, brittlebush, jojoba, lycium, and cheesebush. After 1.2 miles, there are several boulders overlooking the area where the canyon drops off steeply. This is a good place to stop. The Vallecito Stage Station and the Laguna Mountains are visible beyond the canyon mouth. Return the way you came.

Mortero

PICTOGRAPHS
(1.8 miles total; Moderate)

The Blair Valley turnoff is on the east side of S2 at Mile 22.9 (look for the sign approximately 5.7 miles south of Scissors Crossing). Drive east and then south along the base of the hills on the jeep road that goes through the valley. This area has lots of agave, yucca, ocotillo, juniper, and cholla. After 1.2 miles, look for an arrow on a post directing vehicles to go right. Drive another 1.7 miles to a fork and turn left (east). Drive 0.2 mile and turn left again. Drive 2.0 miles to the parking area at the end of the road.

The trail starts at the southern end of the parking area. Follow the trail as it meanders over and around small boulders for 0.2 mile. The next 0.5 mile up to the saddle is through an open area. Look for yucca, mesquite, buckhorn cholla, desert mistletoe, ocotillo, catclaw, juniper, agave, and creosote. After reaching the top of the saddle, walk 0.2 mile down the other side. Look for krameria and hedgehog cactus. The pictographs are on the side of a rock on the right side of the trail. These symbols were painted on the rocks by the Kumeyaay Indians when they lived in the area. Return the way you came.

(ATTEMPTED & ABORTED 12·27·05)

SMUGGLER CANYON OVERLOOK
(2.8 miles total; Moderate)

Follow the driving and hiking directions for Pictographs.

From the pictographs, continue south along the sandy trail for 0.4 mile. Look for sage, indigo, and chuparosa. The trail now enters a narrow canyon with high rock walls. Another 0.1 mile will bring you to the edge of a high drop-off to Smuggler Canyon below. Stay away from the slick rocks at the edge. The Sawtooth Mountains and the Laguna Mountains are visible to the south. Return the way you came.

BOTH TRIPS 1·10·08 w/ CHARLIE

Banded gecko

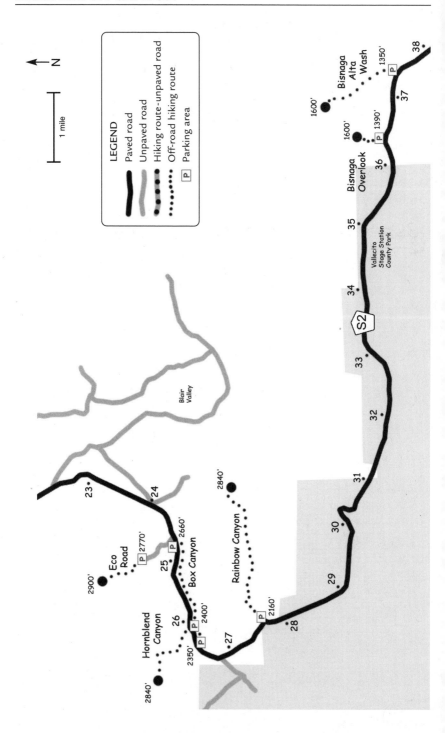

AREA 15
BOX CANYON

This area is higher in elevation than other portions of the Anza-Borrego Desert, supporting a number of plants not seen in the lower elevations.

ECO ROAD
(1.8 miles total; Moderate)

The turnoff is at Mile 24.6 on S2 (approximately 7.4 miles south of Scissors Crossing). Turn right (west) onto the jeep road and drive toward the west for 0.7 mile. Park at the end of the road.

Walk west for 0.1 mile to the rocky hill. Turn right and walk toward the north for 0.2 mile to the sandy wash. (Make a line of rocks across the wash to mark this spot for the return.) Turn right and walk up the wash. Look for juniper, agave, buckhorn cholla, jojoba, yucca, ocotillo, catclaw, hedgehog cactus, barrel cactus, desert mistletoe, and ephedra. After 0.6 mile, the wash forks. This is a good place to stop. Walk back down the wash for 0.6 mile to the line in the sand. Walk up to the top of the low ridge on the left and then walk toward the south. Keep the rocky ridge on the left and the rocky hill on the right. After 0.2 mile, the vehicle should be visible on the left, 0.1 mile away.

BOX CANYON
(1.6 mile one way; Fairly Easy)

The easiest way to do this hike is to arrange a car shuttle, using two vehicles. Drive to Mile 26.3 on S2 (approximately 8.9 miles south of Scissors Crossing). Park in the mouth of the drainage on the left (east) side of S2. Leave one vehicle here. Put all hikers and gear into the second vehicle and drive back up S2 to Mile 24.7 (approximately 1.5 miles north of the first vehicle). Park in the wide area on the north (left) side of S2. Remember to take the keys for the first vehicle.

Walk across S2 to the south side of the road, then continue a few steps more to the California Riding & Hiking Trail. Turn right and follow the CR&HT toward the west as it parallels S2. Look for juniper, catclaw, creosote, yucca, and cholla. After 0.3 mile, the trail enters the canyon. Follow the sandy wash for 0.6 mile to the top of a tall dry waterfall. Bypass the waterfall on the left (south) side, and continue walking to the west in the wash for another 0.7 mile to where the first vehicle is parked. Drive back up S2 to pick up the second vehicle.

HORNBLEND CANYON
(3.6 miles total; Fairly Strenuous)

The parking area is at Mile 26.1 on S2 (approximately 8.8 miles south of Scissors Crossing and just past Box Canyon Monument on the left). There is a small pullout at the bottom of the hill on the east (left) side of the road with enough room for several vehicles.

The canyon entrance is directly across S2 on the west side of the road. Walk across S2 and enter the canyon. Walk in a northerly direction up a narrow, sandy wash with rocky sections. Look for ocotillo, agave, brittlebush, creosote, desert mistletoe, climbing milkweed, desert apricot, buckhorn cholla, hedgehog cactus, juniper, jojoba, ephedra, catclaw, Mason Valley cholla, barrel cactus, prickly pear cactus, desert fir, buckwheat, teddybear cholla, sage, live forever (dudlyea), sugarbush, lycium, fishhook cactus, and yucca. Hornblend is the black rock with brown and gray striations that is seen in this canyon. After 1.1 mile, there is a 10-foot-high dry waterfall, which can be bypassed by walking up the hillside on the left and then over to the wash at the top of the waterfall. Walk another 0.4 mile and then stop and look up the hillside on the left. Tailings from several abandoned mines can be seen. (Do not enter mine tunnels.) Walk another 0.3 mile up the wash to where the canyon opens up on the south (left) side. Walk up the rise on the left side and explore the area. This area was once used by the Kumeyaay Indians, as evidenced by the many morteros (grinding holes) and metates (grinding slicks) in the boulders. Return the way you came.

Roadrunner

RAINBOW CANYON
(4.8 miles total; Strenuous)

The parking area is at Mile 27.6 on S2 (approximately 10.3 miles south of Scissors Crossing). Where the road makes a bend, there is a wide shoulder on the east (left) side with space for several vehicles.

The canyon is directly east of the parking area. Walk toward the canyon mouth. After 0.1 mile, crawl through an old stock fence (which may be removed in the future). Continue up the canyon for another 0.3 mile as it begins to narrow. Look for hedgehog cactus, barrel cactus, beavertail, prickly pear, fishhook, buckhorn cholla, Mason Valley cholla, teddybear cholla, agave, creosote, ocotillo, chuparosa, lycium, desert lavender, and brittlebush. The first dry waterfall is 6-foot high and easy to negotiate. For the next 1.7 miles, the canyon floor alternates between sandy sections and rocky waterfalls. The canyon walls are steep and rocky in most places. This canyon was named for the variety of rock types and colors found along the drainage. Look for ephedra, catclaw, sage, desert apricot, jojoba, buckwheat, juniper, and mesquite. Beyond the dry waterfall made of very white granite, the canyon opens up. Walk toward the east for another 0.3 mile to the top of the saddle. In the distance is Blair Valley. Return the way you came.

BISNAGA OVERLOOK
(1.2 miles total; Fairly Strenuous)

The turnoff is at Mile 36.4 on S2 (approximately 18.8 miles south of Scissors Crossing). Turn left (east) onto a jeep road and drive 0.1 mile to the end of the road and park.

Walk into the wash to the east and turn left. Walk up the rocky canyon for 0.3 mile. Look for chuparosa, ocotillo, creosote, brittlebush, desert lavender, agave, jojoba, barrel cactus, Mason Valley cholla, teddybear cholla, and buckhorn cholla. At the fork, walk to the top of the knoll between the two drainages. Staying near the drainage on the right, walk toward the east for 0.3 mile to the edge of the hill. Enjoy the view of the wide Bisnaga Alta Wash drainage to the east. Return the way you came.

BISNAGA ALTA
(2.8 miles total; Fairly Easy)

The parking area is at Mile 37.3 on S2 (approximately 19.7 miles south of Scissors Crossing). Look for the "Bisnaga Wash" sign on the east (left) side of the paved road. Turn into the dirt parking area behind this sign.

This wash is a drainage from Whale Peak. The bottom of the wash is sandy and very wide. Walk in a northerly direction and then to the northwest, keeping the hills on the left. Look for chuparosa, ocotillo, jojoba, creosote, catclaw, agave, teddybear cholla, Mason Valley cholla, pencil cholla, and barrel cactus. The name *Bisnaga Alta* is Spanish for "tall barrel cactus" that grow in this area. After a 1.4-mile walk, the sandy wash becomes a narrow, rocky drainage that is part of an alluvial fan. This is a good place to stop and explore. Look for fishhook cactus, elephant tree, and cloak fern in the rocky areas. Return the way you came.

Elephant tree

NOTES

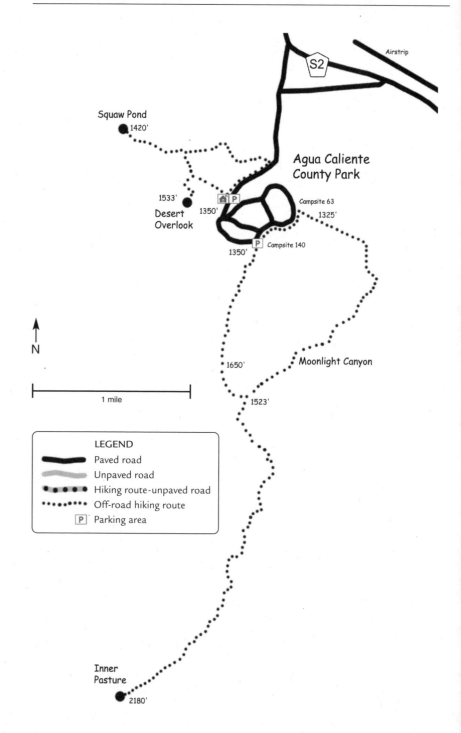

Airstrip

S2

Squaw Pond
1420'

Agua Caliente
County Park

1533'
Desert
Overlook

1350'

Campsite 63
1325'

1350'
Campsite 140

N

1 mile

1650'

Moonlight Canyon

1523'

LEGEND
Paved road
Unpaved road
Hiking route-unpaved road
Off-road hiking route
P Parking area

Inner
Pasture
2180'

AREA 16
AGUA CALIENTE

This area is best known for its geothermal hot springs: the agua caliente, *or hot water. Many visitors come to soak in the warm mineral waters. Operated by San Diego County Parks, Agua Caliente is a popular camping area. Choose between sites with or without hookups, or just visit for the day. The seismic fault that runs under the park creates cracks through which water reaches the surface year-round. This supports the lush vegetation that attracts a variety of birds and other animals.*

To reach the county park, drive to Mile 38.2 on S2 (approximately 21.2 miles south of Scissors Crossing). Turn west (right) at the sign for the park. Drive west for 0.6 mile to the ranger kiosk. This is a fee area. The park is closed during the summer months.

MOONLIGHT CANYON
(1.6 mile loop; Fairly Strenuous)

12.28.07 (BACKWARD) w/ CHARLIE

Drive past the ranger kiosk and through the campground. The trailhead is next to the shuffleboard court on the right and across from site #33. There is an earthquake fault running down the hill toward the parking area. The trail begins at the trail marker next to site #140.

This trail loops around the hill to the south in a counter-clockwise direction and presents the hiker with many rocks and boulders. For the first 0.5 mile, the trail climbs up and over a low hill and then becomes rockier as it ascends to the saddle. The descent is a rocky drop down for 0.2 mile. Look for arrowweed, thornbush, brittlebush, mesquite, catclaw, jojoba, buckhorn cholla, teddybear cholla, agave, ocotillo, creosote, chuparosa, indigo, ephedra, desert lavender, barrel cactus, and coachwhip. The next 0.2 mile descends the rocky and sandy bottom of the wash surrounded by high canyon walls. Then the trail winds through an area with lush vegetation growing where water seeps to the surface. The last 0.4 mile follows the sandy wash as the canyon opens up. The trail ends near sites #63 and #64. Walk straight on the paved road between the two sites and follow the road for 0.2 mile to return to the vehicle.

3.31.08 w/ CHARLIE

INNER PASTURE
(4.4 miles total; Fairly Strenuous)

Follow the driving instructions for Moonlight Canyon (previous page).

Follow the hiking instructions for the first 0.7 mile of Moonlight Canyon. At the bottom of the descent, turn right and walk up the rocky canyon for 0.1 mile. When the canyon forks, look for the faint trail going up the steep hill. Walk up and over this hill for 0.1 mile to another wash. (Make a line in the sand with rocks to mark this spot.) Continue on the trail for another 0.1 mile as it goes over another hill to a wider wash. (Make a second line in the sand with rocks to mark this spot.) Turn right and walk up the sandy, bouldery wash toward the south. After 0.6 mile, take the right fork. Walk another 0.6 mile to the saddle and enjoy the view of the isolated valley known as Inner Pasture. Return the way you came.

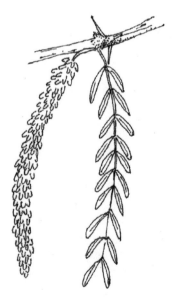

Mesquite leaf and catkin

DESERT OVERLOOK
(0.8 mile total; Strenuous)

The parking area is on the right just before the ranger kiosk and pay station. This hike is within the county park boundaries and payment of the entrance fee is required.

Follow the sign and paved path for the campground circle and continue past the circle area on the trail for 0.1 mile. Look for mesquite, krameria, desert mistletoe, desert holly, brittlebush, agave, ocotillo, indigo, barrel cactus, jojoba, creosote, ephedra, and teddybear cholla. At the junction, go left and ascend for 0.3 mile to the overlook. There are excellent views of the county park to the south, the Carrizo Badlands to the east, and Squaw Pond to the north. Return the way you came.

SQUAW POND
(1.2 mile loop; Fairly Strenuous)

Follow the driving instructions for Desert Overlook.

Follow the sign and paved path for the campground circle and continue past the circle area on the trail for 0.1 mile. Look for mesquite, krameria, desert mistletoe, desert holly, brittlebush, agave, ocotillo, indigo, barrel cactus, jojoba, creosote, ephedra, and teddybear cholla. At the junction with the trail to Desert Overlook, go straight. The next 0.2 mile descends through a sandy and rocky wash. There is a wonderful variety of cactus and desert perennials growing in this area. At the bottom is a trail junction. Turn left and walk 0.2 mile. Look for alkali goldenbush, lycium, saltbush, catclaw, desert mistletoe, desert lavender, chuparosa, and arrowweed. This is a good area to look for birds. The shady area under a huge willow tree is on the edge of Squaw Pond, which is overgrown and hidden by vegetation. This is a good place to stop. Backtrack 0.2 mile to the trail junction. Continue straight ahead down the wash for 0.3 mile. Look for smoketree and desert holly. At the paved road, turn right and follow the road 0.2 mile to the parking area.

It is possible to walk out to Squaw Pond and avoid the steep parts. From the parking area, walk back down the paved road toward S2 for 0.2 mile. Turn left into the wash and walk up it for 0.5 mile to Squaw Pond. Return the way you came. This will add 0.2 mile to the distance and change the difficulty rating to Fairly Easy.

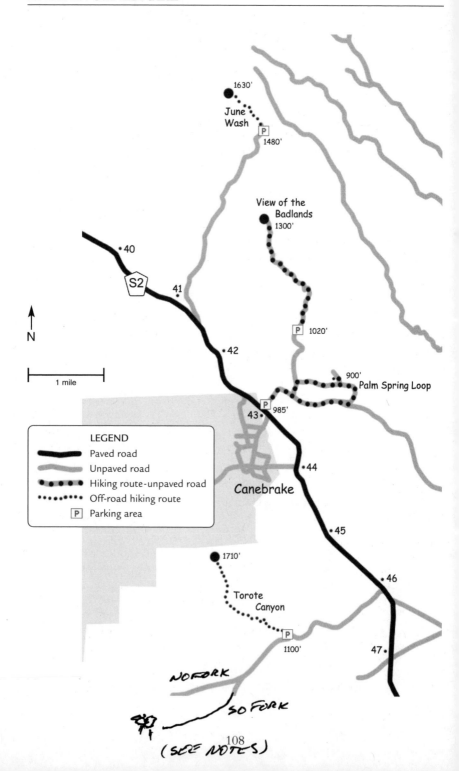

1630'

June
Wash

P
1480'

View of the
Badlands
1300'

•40

S2

41

N

1 mile

•42

P 1020'

900'
Palm Spring Loop

P
43 • 985'

•44

Canebrake

LEGEND
Paved road
Unpaved road
Hiking route-unpaved road
Off-road hiking route
P Parking area

•45

•46

1710'

Torote
Canyon

P
1100'

47 •

NOFORK

SO FORK

(SEE NOTES)

Area 17
Canebrake

The small community of Canebrake is located just west of the state park boundary and about 25 miles south of Scissors Crossing on S2. The community is home to retirees and others who enjoy the quiet of the surrounding desert.

JUNE WASH
(1.2 miles total; Moderate)

The turnoff is at Mile 41.5 on S2 (approximately 23.7 miles south of Scissors Crossing). Turn left (north) and drive 3.5 miles. Park on the side of the road where it is wide enough for another vehicle to pass.

On foot, continue up the narrow jeep road for another 0.3 mile to the end of the road. Continue walking up the narrow, sandy and rocky drainage for another 0.2 mile. Look for smoketree, cholla, indigo, ocotillo, desert holly, and brittlebush. Go left at the fork and walk another 0.1 mile to the top of the ridge. The Carrizo Badlands are visible to the south. Return the way you came.

PALM SPRING LOOP
(3.1 mile loop; Fairly Easy)

The parking area is at Mile 43.0 on S2 (approximately 25.2 miles south of Scissors Crossing). Park on the left (east) side of the road next to the sign for Palm Spring.

Walk along the jeep road toward the east for 0.5 mile. At the fork, continue straight in the wash. This wash is filled with beautiful smoketrees. After 0.4 mile, go left at the fork (there should be a sign for Palm Spring). Follow the jeep road for another 0.5 mile to reach Palm Spring. Nearly 150 years ago, the Butterfield Overland Mail had a stage stop near the spring. Only the historical marker remains now. The spring is nestled into a mesquite thicket with desert mistletoe growing on the trees. When leaving Palm Spring, turn right and follow the jeep road in a westerly direction for 0.3 mile. (Turn right at the junction to make a detour to another mesquite oasis.) Continue straight for 0.7 mile. Look for ocotillo and creosote on the rocky hillside. At the road junction, turn left and walk 0.2 mile. At the main wash, turn right and walk 0.5 mile to return to the parking area.

VIEW OF THE BADLANDS
(5.2 miles total; Fairly Easy)

The turnoff is at Mile 43.0 on S2 (approximately 25.2 miles south of Scissors Crossing). Turn left (east) next to the sign for Palm Spring and drive east on the jeep road for 0.5 mile. Turn left onto another jeep road and drive north for 1.0 mile. Park on the right (east) side of the road, on hard-packed sand, where it is wide enough for another vehicle to pass.

Continue up the jeep road on foot, walking in a northerly direction, as the road follows a sandy wash between eroded mud hillsides. Look for ocotillo, smoketree, creosote, cholla, desert holly, aster, and indigo. After 2.6 miles, the jeep road ends. From the top of the ridge, the Carrizo Badlands are visible to the north and east, and Whale Peak is the mountain to the north. After enjoying the view, return the way you came.

TOROTE CANYON
(4.0 miles total; Fairly Strenuous)

The turnoff is at Mile 46.1 on S2 (approximately 28.3 miles south of Scissors Crossing). Turn right onto the jeep road for Indian Gorge and drive west for 1.7 miles to the parking area on the right, next to the information sign.

Walk into the canyon to the north for 1.3 miles. The sandy canyon floor has many small boulders and several large boulders to negotiate. Look for teddybear cholla, barrel cactus, ocotillo, catclaw, agave, desert lavender, chuparosa, elephant tree, brittlebush, creosote, hedgehog cactus, smoketree, desert mistletoe, and jojoba. When the canyon divides, take the right fork. Continue walking for 0.4 mile to a small valley, and then walk toward the north for another 0.2 mile. At the north end of the valley, walk 0.1 mile up to the saddle. Enjoy the view of the canyon below. Return the way you came.

NOTES

DID LAST 1/2 MILE OR SO OF
← THIS HIKE W/ CHARLIE 12·18·07

DROVE INTO & UP BOTH NORTH & SOUTH
FORKS OF TRAIL INTO INDIAN GORGE
AND TOOK A SHORT HIKE UP TO PALM
GROVE AT THE END OF SO. FK. (2400')
12·30·07   W/ CHARLIE

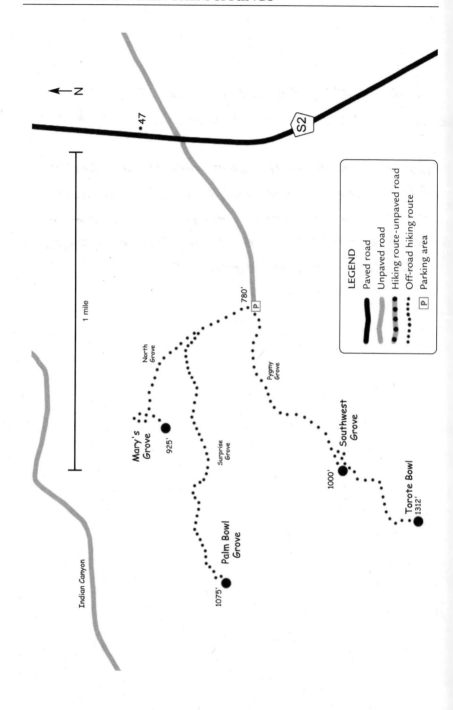

LEGEND
Paved road
Unpaved road
Hiking route-unpaved road
Off-road hiking route
P Parking area

N

S2

·47

780'

1 mile

North Grove

Mary's Grove

925'

Pygmy Grove

Surprise Grove

Southwest Grove

1000'

Torote Bowl

1312'

Palm Bowl Grove

1075'

Indian Canyon

AREA 18
MOUNTAIN PALM SPRINGS

This is a popular area for dry camping. Large groves of the California fan palm, the only native palm to this area, grow in the canyons to the west and north.

All hikes in this section begin from the same parking spot: the turnoff is at Mile 47.1 on S2 (approximately 29.2 miles south of Scissors Crossing). Turn right (west) onto the jeep road and drive 0.4 mile. Go right at the fork and continue for another 0.2 mile. Park in the lot furthest to the west.

SOUTHWEST GROVE
12-20-05
w/ CHARLIE
2-22-11
w/JA COB
(1.4 miles total; Fairly Easy)

From the parking area, walk west past the wooden posts and toward the palm trees. The first 0.3 mile of the trail may be moist from water seeping around Pygmy Grove, the first grove of fan palms. Notice the trunks blackened by past fires. Look for mesquite, desert mistletoe, desert holly, saltbush, buckhorn cholla, ocotillo, and barrel cactus. The next 0.4 mile is drier until the trail reaches Southwest Grove. Look for indigo and brittlebush. The palms trees in this grove also have fire-blackened trunks. Several elephant trees can be seen on the hillside to the north (right). Return the way you came.

TOROTE BOWL
(2.6 miles total; Strenuous)

Follow the hiking directions for the Southwest Grove hike above.

From the middle of the Southwest Grove, look to the south (left) for the rock steps near the bottom of the hill. Follow these steps up and then continue on the trail that switchbacks for 0.2 mile up to the top of the ridge above the palm grove. Look for creosote, desert lavender, ephedra, krameria, and burrobush. There are good views of the Carrizo Badlands to the northeast. At the top, turn right (west) onto the trail to Torote Bowl (signed). Follow the rocky trail for 0.4 mile to the bowl. There are elephant trees scattered all over the rocky hillsides of the bowl. *Torote* is Spanish for elephant tree, which is related to frankincense and myrrh from the Middle East. Return the way you came.

1·22·06
w/ CHARLIE

MARY'S GROVE *(THE HARD) WAY*
(1.4 miles total; Moderate)

If you look north from the parking area, you should be able to see the tops of some palm trees in North Grove. Walk up the wash in a northerly direction toward these trees. After 0.2 mile, the sandy wash gets rocky. Look for catclaw, desert mistletoe, brittlebush, saltbush, creosote, desert lavender, smoketree, mesquite, ocotillo, teddybear cholla, desert holly, and barrel cactus. Walk another 0.3 mile to North Grove. Continue northwest in the drainage for another 0.2 mile to Mary's Grove. Return the way you came.

12·13·07
w/CHARLIE
3 HRS

PALM BOWL GROVE
(2.5 miles total; Moderate)

From the parking area, look north to where the tops of some palm trees are visible. Walk up the wash in a northerly direction toward these trees. Look for catclaw, desert mistletoe, brittlebush, saltbush, creosote, desert lavender, smoketree, mesquite, ocotillo, teddybear cholla, desert holly, and barrel cactus. After 0.2 mile, look for the trail going up the hillside on the left. (The trail may be hidden behind a mesquite tree.) Follow the faint trail for 0.1 mile to the top of the ridge. Walk another 0.5 mile up the wash to Surprise Grove. Look for indigo and chuparosa. Follow the trail through Surprise Grove and walk another 0.4 mile to Palm Bowl. In the past, over 100 palms trees grew here, but many have died or been damaged by fires and storms. Return the way you came.

Datura flower

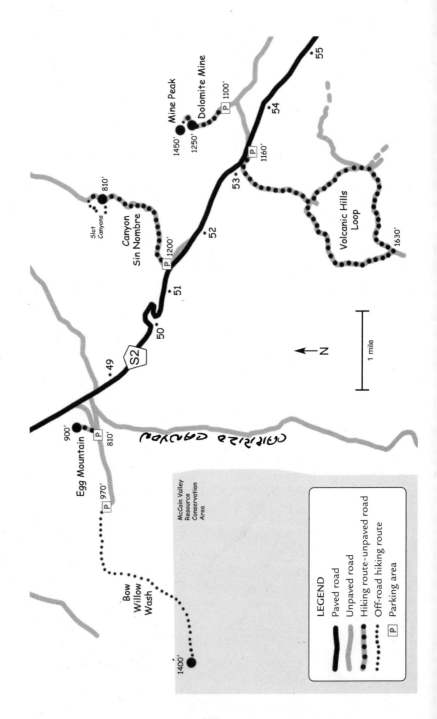

Mine Peak

Dolomite Mine

1450'

1250'

P 1100'

55

54

P 1160'

53

52

51

810'

Slot Canyons

Canyon Sin Nombre

P 1200'

Volcanic Hills Loop

1630'

50'

49

S2

N

1 mile

900'

Egg Mountain

P 810'

CARRIZO CANYON

P 970'

McCain Valley Resource Conservation Area

Bow Willow Wash

1400'

LEGEND

Paved road
Unpaved road
Hiking route-unpaved road
Off-road hiking route
P Parking area

AREA 19
THE SOUTHERN END

This remote area of the Anza-Borrego Desert offers a surprising variety of hikes. Bow Willow, an established primitive campground, is popular during the winter months. Paleontologists have excavated bones from many ancient animals in the Carrizo Badlands.

EGG MOUNTAIN
(0.6 mile total; Fairly Easy)

The turnoff to Bow Willow Campground is at Mile 48.3 on S2 (approximately 30.3 miles south of Scissors Crossing). Turn right onto the jeep road leading to the campground. Drive west for 0.6 mile and then look for the unmarked jeep road on the north (right) side. Park in any wide area.

Walk up the jeep road for 0.3 mile to the top of Egg Mountain. There are 360-degree views of the southern part of Anza-Borrego Desert, including Bow Willow Canyon to the west and the Carrizo Badlands to the northeast. Return the way you came.

BOW WILLOW WASH
(5.6 miles total; Fairly Easy)

The turnoff to Bow Willow Campground is at Mile 48.3 on S2 (approximately 30.3 miles south of Scissors Crossing). Turn right onto the jeep road going to the campground. Drive west for 1.7 miles and park at the end of the road near the wooden posts.

Walk toward the west up the sandy wash. Look for desert willow, ocotillo, mesquite, brittlebush, cheesebush, saltbush, desert lavender, catclaw, barrel cactus, desert mistletoe, smoketree, chuparosa, indigo, agave, jojoba, ephedra, desert apricot, teddybear cholla, and buckhorn cholla. Follow the wash for 2.8 miles to where there are several fan palms near a mesquite thicket. This is a good place to stop. Return the way you came.

1·29·08 @ 2 mi w/ CHARLIE, ED & MARY
(RTN ALONG) + 2 HRS ROCK-CLIMBING

CANYON SIN NOMBRE *(SEE NOTES)*
(3.8 miles or more total; Moderate)

The parking area is at Mile 51.3 on S2 (approximately 33.2 miles south of Scissors Crossing). Turn left (east) onto the jeep road that is signed for Canyon Sin Nombre, which in Spanish means "canyon without a name." Immediately turn to the right and park up on the rise.

From the parking area, follow the jeep road down the hill. The first 1.0 mile goes through an open area with many old ocotillo. Also, look for catclaw, indigo, smoketree, barrel cactus, creosote, saltbush, and brittlebush. The next 3.0 miles follow the jeep road through the canyon. The steep canyon walls have been folded and twisted by past geologic activity. The twisted layers give way to mud and sandstone walls as the canyon opens up. Beautiful smoketrees thrive in this part of the canyon. Many of the side canyons are worth exploring along the way. Stop when you choose, and return the way you came.

2-9-08 (ALONE — *1.5 mi)*

DOLOMITE MINE
(1.2 miles total; Fairly Easy)

The turnoff is at Mile 53.3 on S2 (approximately 35.2 miles south of Scissors Crossing). Turn left (east) onto the jeep road and drive 0.6 mile. Turn left at the intersection and drive 0.2 mile toward the north to a wide parking area on the right. Park here.

Walk along the jeep road toward the north for 0.6 mile to the abandoned mine buildings. Dolomite marble was mined here in the mid-1900s. Look for ocotillo, creosote, barrel cactus, buckhorn cholla, teddybear cholla, agave, desert lavender, catclaw, jojoba, and indigo. Explore the area, then return the way you came.

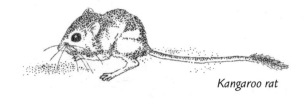

Kangaroo rat

MINE PEAK
(2.0 miles total; Strenuous)

Follow the driving instructions for Dolomite Mine (previous page).

Walk along the jeep road toward the north for 0.6 mile to the abandoned mine buildings. Dolomite marble was mined here in the mid-1900s. Look for ocotillo, creosote, buckhorn cholla, desert lavender, catclaw, jojoba, barrel cactus, teddybear cholla, agave, and indigo. After reaching the mine buildings, turn right and continue walking up the jeep road toward the east for 0.1 mile. At the intersection, turn right and walk 50 feet to the drainage. Make a sharp left turn and continue up the badly eroded jeep road toward the west for 0.1 mile. Continue toward the northeast on the faint trail on the left side of the rockfall. After 0.1 mile, go left at the fork and continue another 0.1 mile up the drainage to the high point on the left. Enjoy the view, then return the way you came.

VOLCANIC HILLS LOOP
(8.2 mile loop; Moderate)

The parking area is at Mile 53.3 on S2 (approximately 35.2 miles south of Scissors Crossing). Turn right (west) into the large parking area near the sign for Jojoba Wash and park.

Follow the jeep road for 1.5 miles. Turn left at the fork to follow the jeep road loop in a clockwise direction. The first 1.0 mile is a bit rocky, then the road drops down into Mortero Wash. (The jeep road that climbs steeply up the other side of the wash leads to Dos Cabezos and is an example of how rough these jeep roads can get.) Turn right and walk up the sandy wash for 0.8 mile to the end of the wash in a box canyon. Backtrack 0.1 mile, turn left, and follow the jeep road as it climbs out of the wash. The road continues around and through the red volcanic hills. This area has many old, large ocotillo, as well as jojoba, barrel cactus, cholla, indigo bush, creosote, and brittlebush. From the top of the wash, follow the jeep road for 1.0 mile to a fork. Turn to the right and follow the road for 2.0 miles to where the loop began. Walk straight for 1.5 miles to return to the parking area.

OTHER HIKES

1-10-06   MICA MINE TRAIL W/CHARLIE
          2.5 - 3.0 mi;

3-17-08   CARRIZO CANYON W/CHARLIE
          2.0 mi

3-24-08   FROM BTM OF CANYON SIN NOMBR
          ALONG OVERLAND TRAIL 2.0 mi
          W/CHARLIE

INFORMATION

Use this Information Section to help ensure that your hike is safe and enjoyable. Included here are tips on what to bring along and what to watch out for. Preparation is vital to your safety in the desert. There are very few established trails in the Anza-Borrego Desert, but with a few precautions you can enjoy the desert safely.

ASSUMPTION OF RISK

As a hiker, you are responsible for your own safety and you assume a certain amount of risk. Do not be afraid to explore the desert, but do be prepared for a variety of situations, and listen to your body so that you can safely enjoy the desert. Trail conditions change constantly, and weather can adversely affect your comfort level. Fitness level, equipment, and preparedness also factor into an outing being safe or becoming a rescue situation. If a hike is beyond your comfort level, turn around. It is more important to return safely to your vehicle so that you can enjoy another hike. than it is to continue beyond your threshold for personal well-being.

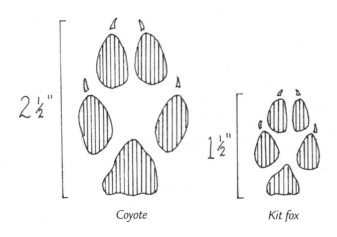

Coyote   Kit fox

PARK REGULATIONS

Anza-Borrego Desert State Park and Aqua Caliente County Park have regulations for protection of the visitors and resources. The basic regulations are listed below. Rules vary between agencies. Contact each park for more specific information.

Everything in the parks is protected. No one may remove or disturb any of the plants, animals, natural features, or cultural artifacts.

All vehicles must be highway legal and must remain on established roads.

Firearms must be unloaded, inoperative, and in a case at all times. (Firearms are not allowed in Agua Caliente County Park.)

Camping is allowed. Contact each park for regulations.

Fires must be confined to metal containers only.

Pets must be on a leash at all times and must be kept inside at night. Pets are not allowed on trails or in the wilderness. (Agua Caliente County Park does not allow pets.)

PARK FEES

Park fees for day use and camping are subject to change.

Contact each park for current information.

HIKING EQUIPMENT

Take the following items with you on any hike:
· sturdy walking shoes
· wide-brimmed hat
· sunscreen
· a daypack to carry everything
· 2-to-4 quarts of water per person per day
· some food or a snack
· first aid kit, including pliers for removing cactus spines
· topographic map of the area
· compass
· whistle
· extra layers (a long-sleeved shirt provides protection from the sun;
  a rain jacket can double as a windbreaker)
· a hiking buddy
· this book
· your common sense

You may want to include these items:
· cell phone
· sunglasses
· binoculars
· walking stick
· field guides for birds, insects, flowers, cacti
· gardening gloves to protect hands when climbing over boulders

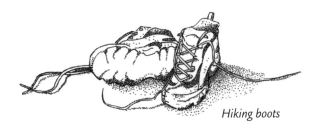

Hiking boots

WEATHER

The desert is known for its heat. Summers can be incredibly hot, with daytime temperatures up to 120°F and nighttime temperatures in the 80s, or sometimes 90s. Add humidity from the summer monsoons, and the weather can be unbearable. Fall and spring are more pleasant with lower daytime temperatures and cool nights. Winters are usually temperate, with average daytime temperatures in the 60s and 70s, and nighttime temperatures in the 40s. However, heat stress can occur in any season. While a person acclimated to the desert may be comfortable hiking in 90°F, someone else may become dehydrated or suffer heat stress or worse when the temperatures are much lower. Heat can be a very real danger at any time of year.

Although the desert is known for its summer heat, winter cold can also be a real danger. By definition, a desert receives less than 12 inches of rain in a calendar year. The desert floor usually doesn't receive much precipitation, but rain and snow are common in the higher elevations during winter storms. Bitter winds can blow off of snow-covered peaks and down over the desert. Add a wind chill factor to temperatures in the 50s and hypothermia becomes a possibility at any elevation. In addition, rain in the high country can bring water gushing down canyons and washes, enabling a storm many miles away to cause flash floods in the desert at any time of year.

Bighorn sheep

PLANTS & ANIMALS

Many people grow up hearing about snakes, tarantulas, and scorpions. In the Anza-Borrego Desert, some of these desert critters are poisonous, but rarely live up to their dangerous reputations. More people have altercations with cholla cactus than with critters.

SNAKES: Many kinds of snakes live in the desert, while only a few are dangerous. All will avoid people if possible. Snakes are active during warmer weather and usually not seen in the cooler winter months. A bite from one of the several species of rattlesnakes in the Anza-Borrego Desert is a very rare event and requires medical attention. Most bites occur when someone tries to handle a snake. By leaving the snake alone, the risk of snakebite is almost nonexistent.

SPIDERS: Tarantulas are big, hairy spiders that look dangerous, but are quite docile. A bite from a tarantula is usually no worse than a bee sting. By only looking at—and not touching—the spider, a bite can be avoided altogether. Tarantulas are seen most often in the fall when males are out looking for females. Black widow spiders are usually seen in warmer months when insects are more abundant. The poisonous female black widow looks like a big black pea with legs and is identified by a red hourglass mark on the underside of the abdomen. The hourglass is easy to see when the female hangs upside-down on the web. If you are bitten by a black widow, seek medical attention as soon as possible, for some people have died from the widow toxin. The brown recluse is also a desert resident. This small nondescript brown spider is usually found around dwellings. The bite is dangerous if left unattended for a few days; antibiotics may be required. Sun spiders look a bit like a scorpion, but don't have the stinging tail. They can give a nasty bite, so again, leave them alone.

SCORPIONS: Scorpions come in all sizes. The tip of the tail contains a poison sac with a stinger attached. Wearing shoes will usually protect your feet from stings. Scorpions are nocturnal and active in the warmer months. The exoskeleton shows up under a black light; turn one on at night and see how many scorpions are sharing the desert with you.

BIGHORN SHEEP: The peninsular bighorn is a desert-adapted subspecies of the bighorn sheep. Rams, ewes, and lambs are frequently seen on rocky outcrops or in the canyons in the northern part of ABDSP.

PLANTS & ANIMALS

MOUNTAIN LIONS: Also known as the "cougar," this big cat is found in the western portions of Anza-Borrego Desert. It preys mainly on bighorn sheep and mule deer and has been known to occasionally attack people. Do not approach or run from a mountain lion. If one approaches you, act big by waving your arms and making a lot of noise.

COYOTES: The desert dog is often seen during the day and heard at night. This animal is well-adapted to the desert and will usually leave people alone. A coyote that has been fed by people will lose its natural fear and approach too closely. Make a lot of noise to scare off any coyote that gets too close. Never feed coyotes or leave food behind.

BIRDS: The desert is a great place for bird watching. Year-round residents include quail, roadrunner, hummingbirds, ravens, thrashers, sparrows, doves, and phoebes. Winter hosts the greatest number of birds, while fall and spring migrations bring unusual species through the area. Water sources are the best places to find birds. Local guidebooks on birding are available.

CACTUS: The teddybear cholla is easily recognized. Spiney balls from this plant tend to stick to shoes and clothes, and then to hands and clothes when trying to remove the balls! Other indigenous cactus include barrel, fishhook, hedgehog, beavertail, prickly pear, and other types of cholla. Spring and early summer is the best time to see cactus in bloom.

OCOTILLO: With its tall, spiny stalks, this odd plant looks like a cactus, but it actually belongs to a different plant family, the Fouquieriaceae. This plant gets most of its moisture through the small leaves grown soon after a rain and then shed only a few weeks later. In spring, flame-colored flowers appear at the tips of the stalks and attract hummingbirds and insects.

AGAVE: Because agave can withstand heat and store water in their fleshy leaves, these succulents are well adapted to the desert. All species flower just once, growing a tall flower stalk at the end of the plant's life span, approximately 20 to 50 years.

PLANTS & ANIMALS

TREES AND SHRUBS: California fan palm is this desert's only native palm. It can be seen in some of the canyons with year-round water, including Borrego Palm Canyon. Palo verde, mesquite, and desert willow are among the desert trees seen in areas with underground water. Smoketree, with its bluish cast to the sage-green leaves, is found in desert washes. Smoketree produces masses of dark blue flowers in May and June. Indigo bush, related to the smoketree, is aptly named for its dark purple flowers that bloom in late spring. Desert lavender and chuparosa are two early-blooming desert shrubs. Creosote bush gives the desert its signature smell after a rain and produces small yellow blooms in spring.

ANNUALS: The Anza-Borrego Desert is known for its springtime annual bloom, but the wildflowers may vary considerably from year to year. In a good year, the desert floor may be carpeted with flowers of many colors. But even when the bloom isn't spectacular on the low desert floor, flowers can usually be found at the higher elevations of the desert and in the mountain canyons where moisture from storms gets trapped.

Jackrabbit

SUGGESTED MAPS

It is always a good idea to take a map when hiking to help orient yourself to the surrounding topography. Because there are very few established foot trails and only a few trail markers to follow in the Anza-Borrego Desert, a map is especially important. Topographical maps from the U.S. Geological Survey are a good resource. Earthwalk Press publishes a "sweat proof" topographic map that covers the entire area included in this book. This and several other maps of the Anza-Borrego Desert State Park area are available in Borrego Springs at the Borrego Desert Nature Center or through the state park. A map of Agua Caliente County Park is available at the park's entrance kiosk or by contacting the county park.

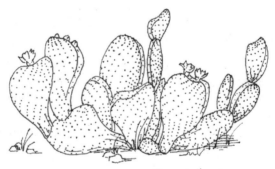

Beavertail cactus

SAFETY TIPS

Planning will increase your safety and comfort.

- For any emergency, call 911.
- Know your physical limitations in any weather.
- Always carry water. Dehydration and heat stress can be life threatening. Two-to-four quarts a day per person is recommended.
- A cell phone will not work in many areas of the Anza-Borrego Desert. You will usually have to get to a high point to get a signal.
- Tell someone where you are going and when you plan to return.
- Always hike with someone.
- Carry a map and use it. Be aware of the terrain and landmarks throughout the hike.
- "Look but don't touch" is a good policy if you are unfamiliar with a plant or animal.
- Don't eat the plants. While some plants are edible, others are poisonous.
- Check the current road conditions with the visitor center at the state park. Road conditions can change as fast as the weather.
- Carry extra water, food, and clothing in your vehicle. Also carry a shovel, tools, and blankets.
- If your vehicle breaks down, stay with it. It is much easier to find a vehicle than a person.
- Snakes, tarantulas, and scorpions are things to be aware of rather than to fear. Don't put your hands where you can't see them. Check out the area before sitting down, and be aware of where you are putting your feet.
- Pack out your trash. "Take only memories and photographs, leave only footprints."
- If you find yourself in trouble, don't panic. Use your common sense, and think the problem through.

Above all, enjoy the desert. It is a very special place for those who explore the area.

CONTACT LIST

Anza-Borrego Desert State Park
200 Palm Canyon Drive
Borrego Springs, CA 92004
Visitor Center: 760-767-4205
Headquarters: 760-767-5311
www.anzaborrego.statepark.org

Agua Caliente County Park
5201 Ruffin Road, Suite P
San Diego, CA 92123-1699
858-694-3049
www.co.san-diego.ca.us/parks

Borrego Springs Chamber of Commerce
P.O. Box 420
Borrego Springs, CA 92004-0420
800-559-5524; 760-767-5555
www.borregospringschamber.com

Anza-Borrego Desert Natural History Association (ABDNHA)
P.O. Box 310, 652 Palm Canyon Drive
Borrego Springs, CA 92004-0310
Office: 760-767-3052
www.abdnha.org

or visit the
Borrego Desert Nature Center
(Operated by the Anza-Borrego Desert Natural History Assn.)
652 Palm Canyon Drive
Borrego Springs, CA 92004-0310
Nature Center: 760-767-3098

Antelope ground squirrel

ACKNOWLEDGEMENTS

A book of this scope requires a lot of time, research, and Band-Aids. Many thanks to all the people who shared their time and knowledge, and special thanks to all my hiking buddies who shared countless adventures in all types of weather and found something interesting around every turn and at the top of every ridge. A big thank you goes to editor Betsy Knaak of ABDNHA, who turned my hiking notes into a book.

—R.H.

ABOUT THE CONTRIBUTORS

Paulette Ache, Illustrator: The small town community, and the Anza-Borrego Desert State Park that surrounds it, attracted Paulette to Borrego Springs in the early 1990s. Her art has been shown in local galleries and at art shows and fundraising events. She enjoys hiking, bird watching, and is a volunteer in the park's paleontology society.

Robin Halford, Author: Robin Halford is a fifth generation Californian who graduated from Colorado State with majors in zoology and entomology. After several years of working in Death Valley in the winter and Yellowstone National Park in the summer, she decided to make a change. In 1990 she discovered Borrego Springs and has never left. An avid hiker, Robin has walked every mile described in this book.

Jef Johnson, Cartographer: Jef has been a devoted Borrego hiker for more than ten years. To accurately reflect the 100-plus hike descriptions, Jef collected GPS data for almost every route. He then relied on twenty years experience in the computer field to convert the field data into maps for use in this book. While following Robin's descriptions, he was delighted to discover some great new hikes in the vast and varied Anza-Borrego Desert.

Scott Mayeda, Book Designer: Scott has been exploring the Anza-Borrego Desert on foot, mountain bike, and 4WD vehicle for more than eighteen years.

INDEX